Traditional Candlewicking

Traditional
Candlewicking

Sandie Meldrum

Kangaroo Press

To my Dad, who died when I was seventeen.
I thank him for buying me my cherished sewing basket when I was ten,
and for always encouraging and loving my hand sewing

Acknowledgments

Many thanks to all the wonderful women who have encouraged my interest in candlewick embroidery. From Northcliffe in the south to Geraldton in the north there are just too many to list. But a special thank you to the Avon Valley women who supported Candlewick Cottage where the inspiration for this book was born.

To Sheila Venn-Brown, Jenny Kirkham and Vivienne Garforth, three special people who gave their advice and enthusiasm willingly—thank you very much.

To my two delightful models, who took the day's shooting in their stride—I was thrilled with the opportunity to have my daughter Jodie model the nightie and be joined by her cousin Rikki in the dress.

To my son Corey for helping collate my first book, and to both my children for their unfailing interest. My apologies to Mum and all those family members who have been sadly neglected.

Many thanks to a dear friend, Gail McLoughlin, for making the lovely porcelain doll, and to Ron and Sylvia for tediously making the miniature pram from matchsticks.

A special thank you to four very important people: Brian Grabsch for his graphic designs and illustrations; he was put under pressure and took it in his stride. Jason James for his photography. A very talented young man, I am pleased I found him, he knew exactly what I wanted. Gail Rogers for her calming influence and superb flair for creating photographic settings—also to her husband and family for tolerating the invasion of their beautiful home. My 'sister', Judi Oliver, for taking over the responsibility for the dreaded task of typing. Thank you all for the support as the deadline approached.

My most affectionate thanks are to my partner Brian for his patient help and tolerance when my thoughts were a million miles away, and for his tolerance of my impatient moments when I was reading and correcting my material.

Reprinted in 1996 and 1998
First published in 1993 by Kangaroo Press
an imprint of Simon & Schuster Australia
20 Barcoo Street East Roseville NSW 2069
Printed in Hong Kong through Colorcraft Ltd

ISBN 0 86417 564 7

Contents

Introduction

Candlewicking is a form of embroidery which originated in America in the early 1800s. Museums throughout America display collections of bedcovers called candlewick spreads. The design on a candlewick spread was formed by elaborate embroidery, the most popular stitches being the colonial knot, French knot and stem stitch, worked in white on a white background.

The thread used originally was the cotton twist yarn used in candle making. Over the years materials have changed; there is still a cotton available that resembles the wick thread, but most people now use a knitting or crochet cotton or stranded cotton.

The pioneer women were very limited in their choice of fabrics, using mostly handwoven muslin or 100% cotton as the basis for their work. These traditional fabrics are still used, though today they are of a better quality.

Until quite recently candlewicking was a dying art in America, but since the early 1980s has experienced a popular revival. Embroiderers in South Africa and Australia discovered this wonderful needle art just a couple of years later.

With the American revival came a widened array of stitches and the introduction of colour. It is very rewarding to create new designs by changing stitches but I'm still out on the question of colour—to my mind nothing is more elegant than the traditional cream on cream that was used in the 1800s.

Colonial women would lend each other their quilts to copy designs. This was done by placing the new fabric on top of the borrowed quilt and rubbing the surface lightly with a cast iron pot. The iron from the pot would form a black pattern on the fabric. Today's modern tools make transferring so much easier.

Candlewicking can be very enjoyable and relaxing. Women as young as eight and eighty have learned to candlewick and found endless hours of pleasure.

The designs in this book range from beginners to advanced. There is no limit to the projects that can involve candlewicking—just because I haven't included a particular item here doesn't mean it can't be done.

Equipment and Fabrics

Fabric preparation

Choosing fabrics

America's pioneer women worked their candlewick designs on 100% cotton and muslin fabrics. Once the embroidery was completed they washed the fabric in very hot water, causing the fabric to shrink and the stitches to tighten. This shrinking process gave a puckered look and made the stitches and knots stand out prominently.

The fabrics used today, calico and homespun, are available in both unshrunk and preshrunk form. Both are available seeded and unseeded; used in conjunction with wadding, they give modern work the same appearance as the pioneer pieces.

When selecting fabric, especially the large amount needed for a quilt, be sure to purchase sufficient from the one bolt, because there are dye-lot differences in all fabrics. The differences can be very noticeable, and very disappointing, on your treasured quilt.

Use of a wadding behind the fabric provides a further dimension to the candlewick technique. While the candlewick technique itself causes the stitches and knots to stand out, the use of wadding further accentuates them by raising the fabric where desired. The use of wadding also helps to camouflage your underwork of stitches. Wadding is also used in an Italian embroidery technique called *trapunto*.

Cotton lace

It is important to preshrink cotton lace before attaching it to a project.

Wash the lace in warm soapy water, then rinse it thoroughly in cold water. Don't use really hot water, as it may cause over shrinkage. Iron the lace dry with a warm iron. This can be a tedious job but it is well worth the effort as lace can be an expensive part of your quilt.

Unshrunk calico or homespun

Soak the fabric overnight in a bath of cold water (please don't use washing powders). This process will release the dressings and starch and soften the fabric. Using hot water tends to 'cook' the starch, resulting in fabric which looks patchy in places.

The next day wash the fabric in warm soapy water, by hand or in the washing machine, then rinse in cold water. The creases are easier to remove if the fabric is ironed while still damp.

Preshrunk calico or homespun

Preshrunk fabric doesn't need to be soaked overnight, but otherwise is treated the same. Wash it by hand or in the washing machine in warm soapy water, rinse in cold water. The creases are easier to remove if fabric is ironed while still damp.

Wadding

Sewing enthusiasts are fortunate in having a huge range of wadding to select from, in wool, polyester and cotton.

Polyester wadding is gauged by weight; in this book I have used 100 g apparel wadding for small projects and cushions. Pelon is a polyester wadding especially suitable for table cloths and table runners.

Wool wadding is available in 100% wool or mixed with polyester in various proportions depending on the brand. Wool and wool mixes are suitable for quilts.

Cotton wadding is not usually suitable for candlewicking as stitching must be worked very closely to prevent the wadding fibres breaking up.

Needles

Sharp, large-eyed needles are the most suitable for candlewicking, the No. 6 Crewel embroidery needle being my preference. They can be purchased in a packet of ten. The No. 22 Chenille needle is also suitable.

Threading a needle

The thickness of the thread used in candlewicking can sometimes make threading the needle difficult. I find it helps to wet the tip of the cotton, then flatten the tip with your teeth. This creates a fan-shape, spreading the strands and making threading the needle so much easier.

Work with a maximum of 40 cm of cotton—any longer and the eye of the needle tends to fray the cotton, even causing it to lose its sheen. This is more noticeable on satin and with fishbone stitch.

I find it helpful to thread 4 or 5 needles at a time. This gives a good steady flow of work, leading to greater consistency. Make a knot at the end of the thread.

Threads

The special candlewicking thread used in America is not always available on the Australian market. Knitting or crochet cotton is a suitable substitute and is available in a large range of thicknesses. Embroidery cottons can also be used but I prefer 100% Pellicano cotton No. 5 in pearl sheen. I also like DMC Pearlé thread, which is also available in a large range of thicknesses.

An embroidered article can look stunning with the addition of varied shades and thicknesses. It's fun to experiment with all types of cottons. Both DMC and Pellicano carry a lovely range of pastel colours, which are becoming more popular in candlewicking. I still feel, however, that nothing is more elegant than the traditional cream on cream that was used in the 1800s.

Tracing the designs

Note: To fit as many designs as possible into this book, it became necessary in some cases to provide only a quarter or a half of a design. Trace the complete design onto tracing paper, following the instructions on the pattern. I suggest pinning the completed pattern to your fabric.

To position a pattern accurately you usually need to find the centre of the fabric. Fold it in half horizontally and then vertically. Press your fingernail across the folds to create crease marks.

The design can be transferred onto the fabric in three ways:

1. If the fabric is fine the design can be easily seen, and traced by pinning fabric and design together with the creases and arrows aligned.
2. Sticky-tape both design and fabric to a window and trace, using the sun as a light source.
3. Use a glass-topped table, or rest a piece of glass on top of blocks, and place a torch or bedside lamp underneath the glass. Place the design and fabric on top, sticky-tape both in place and trace.

A blue water-soluble marking pen is suitable for tracing the designs onto the fabric as the colour is easily removed after the project is completed. *Cold water* should be used to remove the markings as warm water will cause the ink to become permanent.

The patterns which appear in this book incorporate horizontal and vertical arrows which can be matched to the creased lines on your fabric.

Using the hoop

Holding the hoop

The hoop should always be used in candlewicking with the fabric taut to give evenness to the work. Moving the hoop around to different working positions will not harm your stitch work.

Hold the hoop in your left hand, using your fingers like a pair of scissors. Your pointing finger and thumb are on the top of the hoop (front view). These two fingers hold the thread and control the tension. The other fingers at the back of the hoop are used to support the fabric (back view). Thumb and first finger on top of the hoop is important when making the colonial and French knots. It will feel very uncomfortable at the start, but persevere. The other stitches allow you to have four fingers underneath with the thumb on top of the hoop to hold the thread down if necessary.

Most designs in this book require a 20 cm (8'') embroidery hoop. Smaller projects call for a 10 cm (4'') hoop.

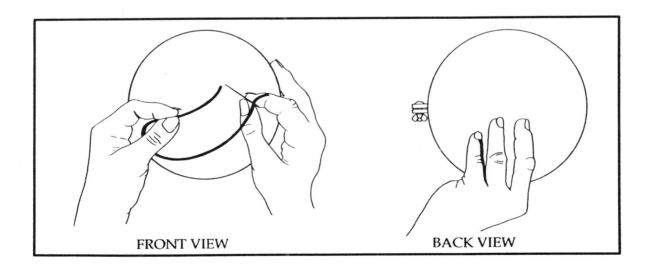

FRONT VIEW   BACK VIEW

Stitches and how to sew them

Unravelling twists

Working colonial and French knots tends to create twists in the cotton. When this happens, turn your project upside down and let the needle and cotton hang down until the twist has unravelled. Run your finger and thumb down the cotton to help speed up the process.

1. Stem/outline stitch

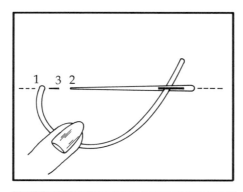

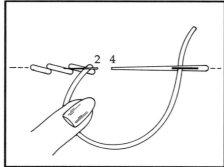

This stitch is used on curves and for outlining designs.

Working from left to right, bring the needle up at 1; following the line of the design, insert the needle at 2 and come up at 3 (half the length of the stitch), holding the thread down with the left thumb. Insert the needle at 4 and bring it up at 2. Continue in this way, keeping the stitches even. Make the stitches smaller on the sharp curves.

2. Fishbone stitch

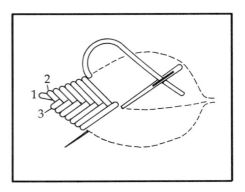

This stitch looks great on leaves, hearts, and as a fill-in on small shapes. Bring the thread up at 1, and make a small straight stitch down the centre line of the shape. Bring the needle up at 2, and slope down to the centre line at the base of the first stitch. Bring the thread up at 3, and back at an angle to the centre, slightly overlapping the previous stitch. Work the stitches evenly and close together. Continue working in this way, on alternate sides, until the shape is filled in.

3. Up and down buttonhole

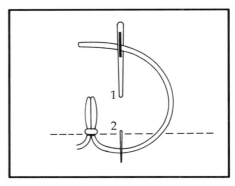

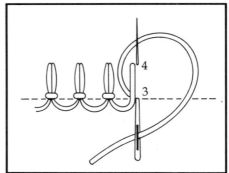

This variation of buttonhole stitch looks very attractive around curves and circles. These stitches look effective from about 5 mm to 15 mm apart. Starting with the thread on the lower line, insert the needle at 1 and bring it through at 2, with the needle vertical and keeping the thread under the needle point. Pull the thread through to form a loop. Insert the needle vertically at 3 and bring up at 4, very close to the first stitch. Keeping the thread under the needle point, pull the thread through, pulling first in an upward direction, then downwards. This will form pairs of vertical stitches crossed by a small bar.

4. Colonial knot

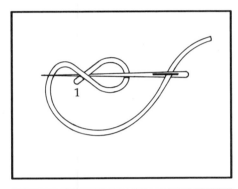

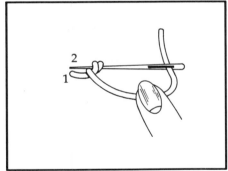

Bring the needle up in the centre of the dot. Hold the cotton lightly between thumb and forefinger of the left hand. Working the stitches from left to right, place the needle under the thread and then twist it around to the left and under the thread so that a figure of eight is formed. Pull the thread taut with the left hand and insert the needle back into the fabric on the right hand side of the thread (2), close to where it came up, at the same time pulling the thread firmly with the left thumb and forefinger. These two fingers control the tension. This stitch is the most widely used in a candlewicking and has the appearance of a small rosebud.

5. Herringbone stitch

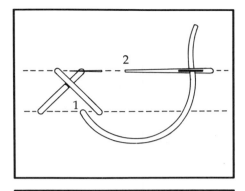

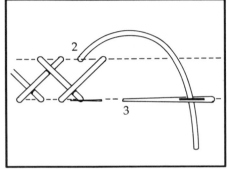

This stitch is effective, closed or open, for borders and filling in spaces. Working between two lines, bring the needle out on the lower left side at 1, insert the needle on the upper line a little to the right, and take a small stitch (2); insert the needle on the lower line a little to the right and take a small stitch to the left (3). Repeat, alternately, on the upper and lower lines, keeping the stitches evenly spaced.

6. Straight stitch

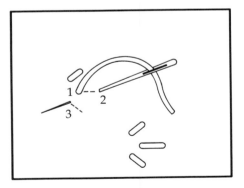

A quick and easy way of working flowers, stars and leaves or petals. Draw the thread up at 1, insert the needle at 2 and out at 3, drawing the thread through.

7. Satin stitch

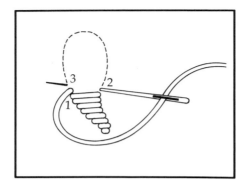

Draw thread up at 1, insert needle under at 2, up at 3 and draw thread through, working stitches close enough to fully cover the shape without overlapping strands.

Since long satin stitches can become loose and untidy, only small shapes should be attempted.

8. Coral stitch

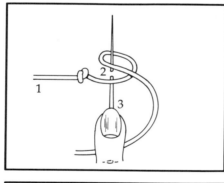

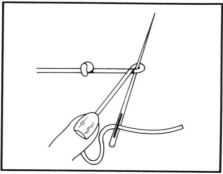

This stitch may be used as a filling or for the veining of leaves, outlines etc. It is more comfortable when using a hoop to work from left to right.

Bring thread through at the end of the line to be

covered. Take a small portion of the material with the needle (2), hold the needle down with left thumb (3), twist the thread over, then under the needle from right to left (diagram A). Hold thread taut with left thumb (diagram B), and pull the needle through. The stitch is varied by the angle of the needle and the spacing of the knots.

9. Feather stitch

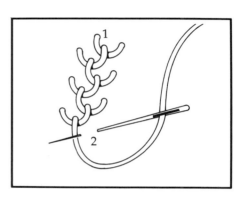

This stitch looks great on the veins of butterflies, and is a quick filler on curves and straight lines.

Bring the thread up at the beginning of the centre line (1), take a stitch a little to the right of the line and at an angle (2), as shown in diagram.

Pull the needle through over the working thread. Take a stitch a little to the left of the line and at an angle, pull the needle through over the working thread.

Continue working in this way, alternately to right and to left.

10. Fly stitch

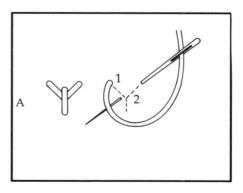

Fly stitch looks effective in small hearts and curved lines with the stitches close together (diagram B).

Bring the thread up at the top of the left arm of

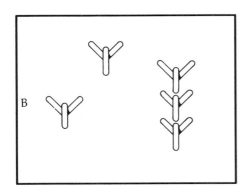

An alternative is to work a cross-stitch on all intersections (C).

12. Chain stitch

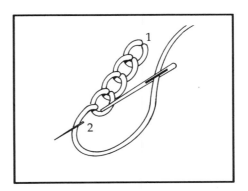

the V (1), insert needle at right arm of the V, take a small stitch downwards to the centre of V (2).

Pull the needle through over the working thread, insert the needle just below the point where it came up, so that a small stitch is formed tying down the previous thread.

The final 'tying' stitch may be varied in length to produce different effects.

11. Trellis stitch

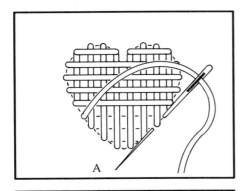

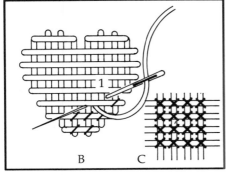

This is very effective as a border stitch.

Bring the thread out at the top of the line (1), and form a loop with it. Insert the needle into the exact spot where the thread emerged and bring it out a short distance below (2). Draw the needle through over the loop of working thread.

Try and keep the chain loops at equal lengths.

13. French knot

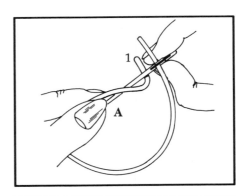

This stitch makes a good filler on baskets, hearts and open designs.

Fill the area with long evenly spaced stitches, across the space horizontally and vertically (A).

Stitch all intersections down with a small slanting

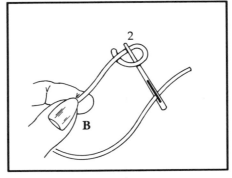

The French knot is used where a finer knot than the Colonial knot is required.

Bring thread up in the centre of the dot (1); hold the cotton lightly between thumb and forefinger of left hand (A). Working the stitch from right to left, place the needle under the thread and then twist it around to the right. Insert the needle back into the fabric where it came up (2), at the same time pulling the thread firmly with the left thumb and forefinger (B). These two fingers control the tension.

14. Double lazy daisy

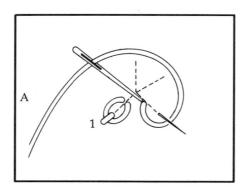

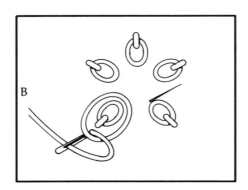

This can be formed in groups to make flower petals, be used singly on stems to simulate leaves, and may be worked in two colours.

Follow the instructions for chain stitch (A), but anchor each loop at the foot with a small stitch (1).

On completion of your flower repeat the procedure with a larger stitch outside the first (B).

15. Couching

This stitch gives a raised rope effect and looks great on straight stems and the midvein of a leaf (D).

The threads are laid on top of the fabric then tied down with small stitches. Bring needle up at A 1,

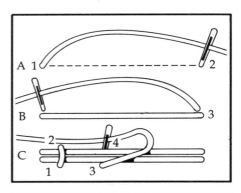

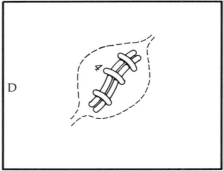

and down at 2. Bring thread up above 2 at B 3 and take back down above 1.

Now secure the threads with small tie-down couching stitches as in C, taking care not to pull the tie-down stitches too tightly. Bring needle up at 1, down at 2, then up at 3 and down at 4. Continue in same manner across laid area, spacing the tie-down stitches evenly.

16. Buttonhole stitch

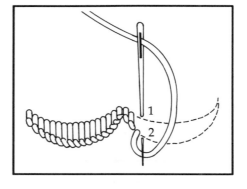

This can be used for floral forms, borders and scalloping.

Starting with the thread coming up on the lower line, insert the needle at 1 and bring it through at 2, with the needle vertical and keeping the thread under the needle point. Pull the thread through to form a loop and repeat, working the stitches close together.

Mitred corners

Hemming

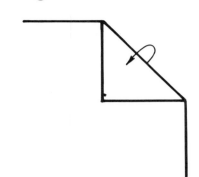

Figure 1

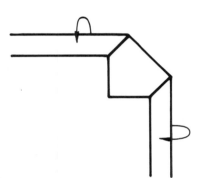

Figure 2

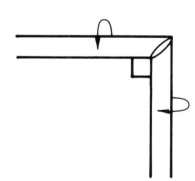

Figure 3

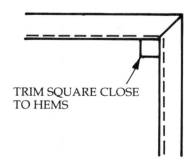

TRIM SQUARE CLOSE
TO HEMS

Figure 4

To make a neatly finished hem around a table cloth, mitre all four corners and hem as follows.

Fold each corner of the fabric, wrong sides together, 10 mm (½'') toward the centre of the fabric (Figure 1). Make a hem around all four edges of the cloth by turning each edge under 5 mm (¼''), pressing as you go (Figure 2), and then another 5 mm (¼''), also pressing as you go (Figure 3). Pin, tack and machine stitch. Trim out the small squares left in the corners very close to the hem (Figure 4).

Mitring lace to a hemmed edge

Place lace wrong side to the right side of the fabric, 5 mm (¼'') in from the edge of the hemmed fabric. Machine stitch, stopping 5 mm (¼'') from the corner (Figure 5).

Measure the width of your lace—say it's 3 cm (1¼''). Turn lace back on itself for 3 cm (1¼'') from the machined stopping point (Figure 6). Stitch from that point to the lace corner on the diagonal, on the wrong side of the lace (Figure 6), taking care

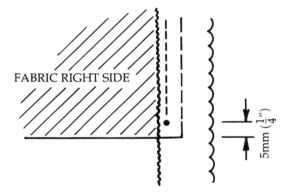

FABRIC RIGHT SIDE

5mm ($\frac{1}{4}$'')

Figure 5

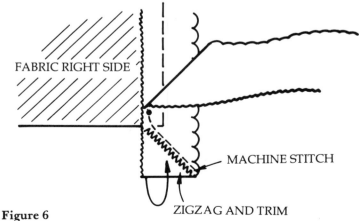

FABRIC RIGHT SIDE

MACHINE STITCH

ZIGZAG AND TRIM

Figure 6

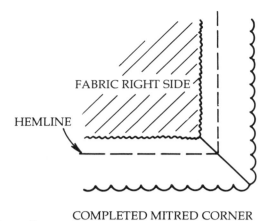

FABRIC RIGHT SIDE

HEMLINE

COMPLETED MITRED CORNER

Figure 7

not to catch the fabric corner. Zigzag close to machine stitching, trim close to the zigzag. Fold lace back and continue around the corner on the other edge (Figure 7).

Making a ruffle and cushion

These instructions can be followed for a square cushion of any size but will have to be adapted for round or rectangular cushions. You will need, besides the candlewicked cushion front, matching fabric for the back and the ruffle, a backing layer of light wadding to go behind the candlewicked front, a cushion filler, and a zip long enough to allow insertion of the filler.

Ruffle and lace

1. To make a ruffle, first stitch the fabric strips together to make one long ruffle. They can easily be sewn together with straight 5 mm (¼ '') seams, placing right sides together. Press seam open to evenly distribute the thickness of the seam (Figure 1). Sew a seam at the end to make the strip into a loop (Figure 2).
2. Fold the ruffle in half longways, wrong sides together, and press (Figure 3). Fold the loop to divide it in half and mark these points with pins (Figure 4). Fold each half in half again to divide into quarters, and mark these points with pins (Figure 5). This helps when you come to gather the ruffle, as it is easier to gather each quarter separately. These marks can also be used to position the ruffle evenly on the cushion top.
3. Lace can be gathered with the ruffle. Join seams on lace to make a loop, neatening seams with a small zigzag. Place lace onto ruffle, aligning raw edge of lace with cut edges of ruffle, and pin together with the divider pins.

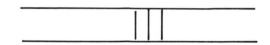

Figure 1

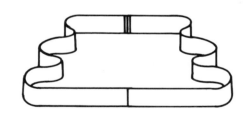

Figure 2

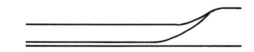

Figure 3

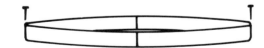

Figure 4

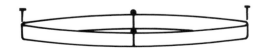

Figure 5

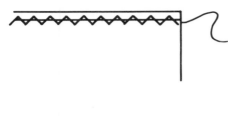

Figure 6

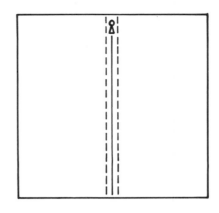

Figure 8

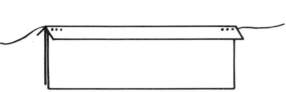

Figure 7

4. The following method is very helpful for gathering ruffles. Set your sewing machine for the longest, widest zigzag stitch. Lay a piece of heavy thread or candlewicking cotton 3 mm (⅛'') from the cut edges of the ruffle; zigzag over this thread, being careful not to stitch into it (Figure 6). This thread can then be pulled easily to gather the ruffle.

5. Gather ruffle, one quarter at a time, to match the sides of the cushion. Pin, right sides and raw edges together, to the cushion front. Distribute gathering evenly, making sure extra gather is added to corners to avoid a 'pulled' appearance.

6. Use large stitches to tack top of ruffle onto cushion. Machine stitch on raw edges, allowing a 5 mm (¼'') seam around the four sides.

Zipper back

1. With right sides together, machine stitch the long edges of the two pieces of cushion back together, making a 10 mm (½'') seam (Figure 7). Press seam open. Sew zipper in place under the seam following the manufacturer's instructions (Figure 8). Cut first seam open to expose zipper.

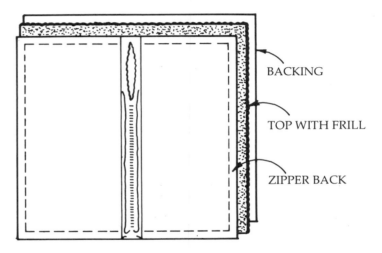

BACKING

TOP WITH FRILL

ZIPPER BACK

Figure 9

2. Place backing wrong side up, cushion top right side up and zippered back wrong side up (Figure 9). Pin and tack all layers together. Stitch a 5 mm (¼'') seam around all four sides. Zigzag or overlock around seams and remove tacking thread. Turn the cushion cover right side out through zipper opening and insert cushion filler.

17

THE FAMILY ROOM

Illustrated on page 34

Wall Hanging

Materials

Note: Before cutting fabric and lace wash following instructions on page 7.

calico or homespun for front and back of wall hanging, 2 pieces 53 cm × 45 cm (21" × 17¾")
calico or homespun for loops, 10 cm × 56 cm (4" × 21")
apparel wadding, 53 cm × 45 cm (21" × 17¾")
flat cotton lace, 2.30 m × 25 mm (2¼ yd × 1")
tracing paper
curtain rod or dowel suitable for hanging

1. Fold the fabric front piece in half horizontally and then vertically, pressing your fingernail across the folds to create crease marks. The patterns that appear in this book have horizontal and vertical arrows which you match to the crease lines on your fabric.
2. Fold the tracing paper in the same manner as the fabric and draw faint lines on these creases. This centres the paper. Place the paper over the parts of the design on pages 21–23, matching the arrows. Trace onto the paper. Pin fabric and paper together and transfer the design from the tracing paper onto the front fabric piece with a blue water-soluble marking pen, following the instructions on page 9. Tack the wadding to the wrong side of the front fabric, place in a hoop and pull the fabric taut.
3. Work the candlewick embroidery on the front fabric piece.
4. When complete wash out the blue pen markings with cold water. Allow the fabric to dry, then press carefully with a warm iron.
5. Place the flat lace on the wall hanging so that the raw edges are together, and the wrong side of the flat lace and the right side of the wall hanging are together. Pin and tack together. Mitre the corners following instructions on page 15.
6. Tack and machine stitch the inside edge of the flat lace, i.e. the scalloped edge, to the wall hanging.
7. Fold the 10 cm × 56 cm (4" × 21") strip of fabric in half lengthwise, right sides together. Stitch 5 mm (¼") in from raw edges, turn through and press. Cut into four lengths of 14 cm (5½") for the wall hanging loops.
8. Fold the loops in half and match their raw edges with that of the fabric. Pin and tack them in position as shown in the diagram.
9. With right sides together pin and tack the backing fabric to the front fabric and stitch 5 mm (¼") in from all raw edges, leaving a 12 cm (5") opening at the bottom for turning.
10. Zigzag or overlock edges. Clip the corners and remove tacking. Turn right side out.
11. Fold the raw edges at the opening 5 mm (¼") inside the hanging and press to create a neat seam. Neatly slip stitch the opening closed.
12. Remove all remaining tacking and press carefully.

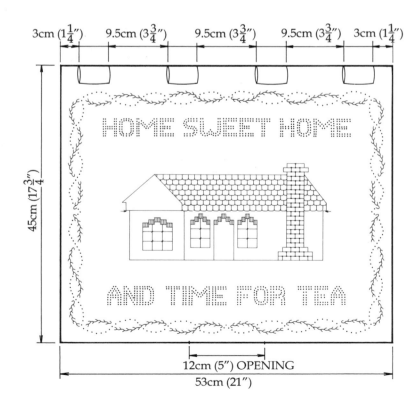

Wall hanging design

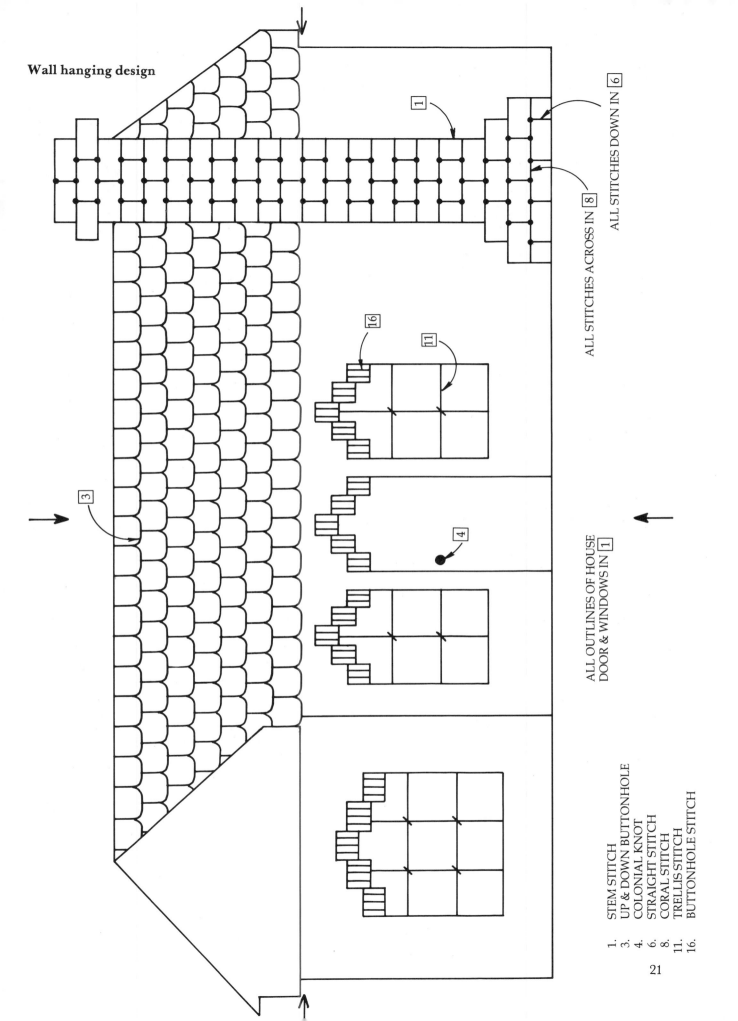

ALL STITCHES DOWN IN 6

ALL STITCHES ACROSS IN 8

ALL OUTLINES OF HOUSE
DOOR & WINDOWS IN 1

1.   STEM STITCH
3.   UP & DOWN BUTTONHOLE
4.   COLONIAL KNOT
6.   STRAIGHT STITCH
8.   CORAL STITCH
11. TRELLIS STITCH
16. BUTTONHOLE STITCH

21

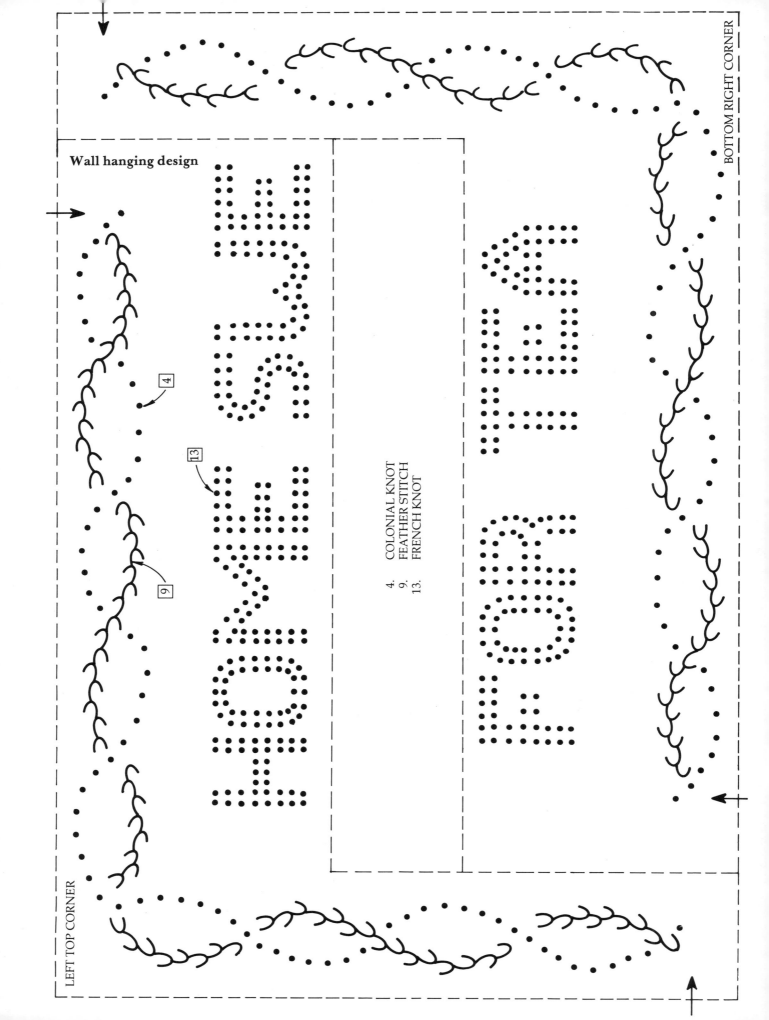

Wall hanging design

BOTTOM RIGHT CORNER

LEFT TOP CORNER

4. COLONIAL KNOT
9. FEATHER STITCH
13. FRENCH KNOT

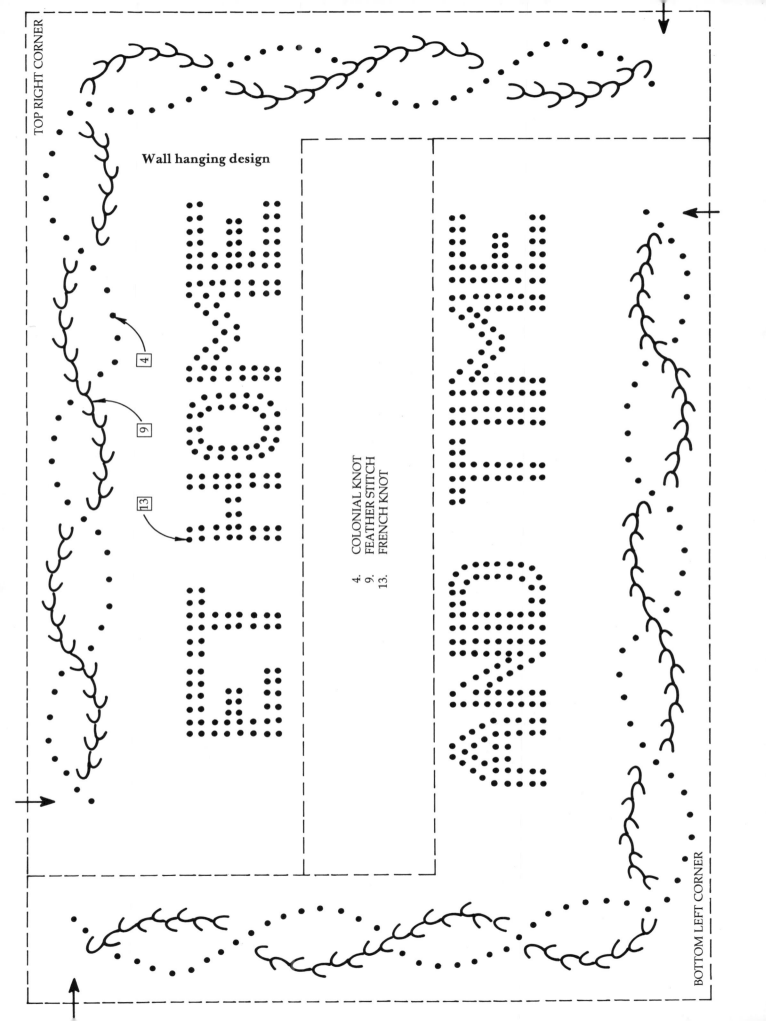

TOP RIGHT CORNER

Wall hanging design

4

9

13

COLONIAL KNOT
FEATHER STITCH
FRENCH KNOT

4.
9.
13.

BOTTOM LEFT CORNER

Illustrated on page 34

Doll's Pram Quilt

Materials

Note: Before cutting the fabric and lace wash following instructions on page 7.

calico or homespun for front and back, 2 pieces
   34 cm × 44 cm (13½'' × 17½'')
apparel wadding, 34 cm × 44 cm (13½'' × 17½'')
gathered lace, 1.60 m × 2 cm (1¾ yd × ¾'')
insertion lace, 1 m × 10 mm (1 yd × ½'')
flat lace, 2 m × 15 mm (2¼ yds × ⅝'')
satin ribbon, 1 m × 5 mm (1 yd × ¼'')
tracing paper

1. Trace the design on page 26 onto tracing paper.
2. Fold the fabric front piece in half horizontally and then vertically. Press your fingernail across the folds to create crease marks. Matching the crease marks to the arrows, pin the fabric and paper together.
3. Transfer the design from the tracing paper onto the front fabric piece with a water-soluble blue marking pen, following the instructions on page 9. Tack the wadding to the wrong side of the front fabric. Place the front piece in the hoop and pull the fabric taut.
4. Work the candlewick embroidery on the front fabric piece.
5. When complete wash out blue pen markings in cold water. Allow the fabric to dry then press carefully with a warm iron.

6. To create a very special effect, join the flat lace to the insertion lace. Cut the 15 mm (⅝'') flat lace in half and butt the edges of the flat lace and the insertion lace together so they can be joined (Figure 1). Zigzag together (Figure 2). The width setting of your machine should enable the needle to encompass both pieces of the lace heading.
   N.B. All lace headings are *not* the same. Settings will have to be adjusted to suit headings on the lace used. The length of your stitch should be fairly short.
   Butt the other half of the lace to the other side of the insertion lace, and zigzag (Figure 3). Press carefully with a warm iron.
7. Position the lace on an angle on two corners of the quilt, starting 15 cm (6'') from the corner (Figure 4); pin, tack and machine stitch in place.
8. Pin the gathered lace, right sides and raw edges together, right around the front of the quilt. Distribute gathering evenly, making sure extra gather is added to corners to avoid 'pulled' corners.
9. With right sides together, pin and tack the backing fabric to the front fabric. Stitch 5 mm (¼'') in from all raw edges, leaving a 12 cm (4¾'') opening at the bottom for turning.
10. Zigzag or overlock seams, clip corners and remove tacking. Turn right side out.
11. Fold the raw edges at the opening 5 mm (¼'') inside the quilt, and press to create a neat seam. Neatly slip stitch the opening closed. Remove all remaining tacking and press carefully with a warm iron.

JOINING FLAT LACE TO INSERTION LACE

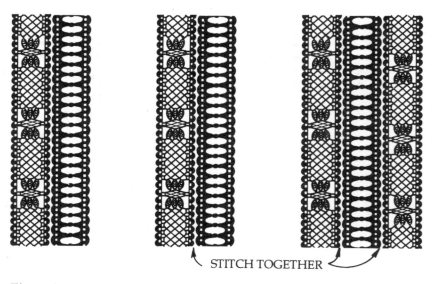

STITCH TOGETHER

Figure 1   **Figure 2**   **Figure 3**

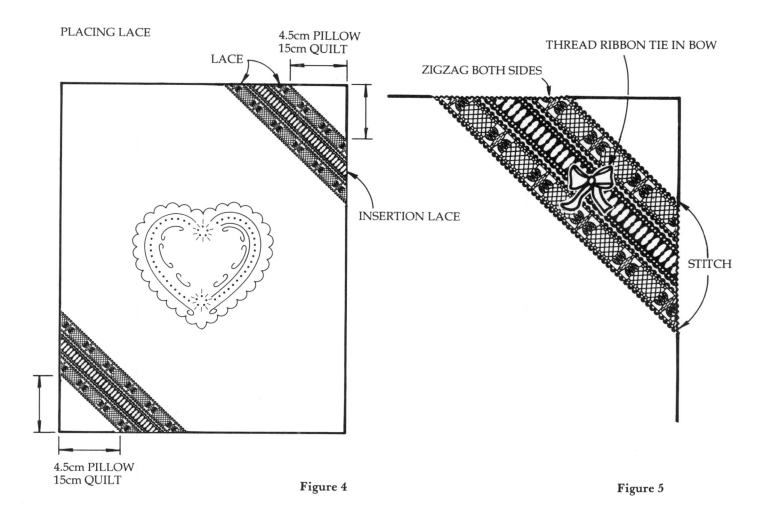

PLACING LACE

LACE

4.5cm PILLOW
15cm QUILT

INSERTION LACE

4.5cm PILLOW
15cm QUILT

Figure 4

ZIGZAG BOTH SIDES

THREAD RIBBON TIE IN BOW

STITCH

Figure 5

Doll's Pram Pillow

Illustrated on page 34

Materials

Note: Before cutting the fabric and lace wash following instructions on page 7.

calico or homespun for front and back, 2 pieces 29.5 cm × 14 cm (11¾″ × 5½″)
apparel wadding, 29.5 cm × 14 cm (11¾″ × 5½″)
gathered lace, 95 cm × 2 cm (37½″ × ¾″)
insertion lace and flat lace (left over from Doll's Pram Quilt)
satin ribbon, 40 cm × 5 mm (15¾″ × ¼″)
polyester stuffing
tracing paper

1. Trace the design on page 26 onto tracing paper.
2. Follow instructions 2–6 for Doll's Pram Quilt.
3. Position the prepared flat lace and insertion lace on two corners of the pillow, starting 4.5 cm (1¾″) from the corner (Figure 4). Pin, tack and machine stitch in place.
4. Follow instructions 8–10 for Doll's Pram Quilt. Remove all remaining tacking on the pillow. Press carefully with a warm iron. Fold the raw edges at the opening 5 mm (¼″) inside the pillow and press to create a neat seam.
5. Fill the opening carefully with stuffing, making sure to push stuffing firmly into the corners.
6. Neatly slip stitch the opening closed.

25

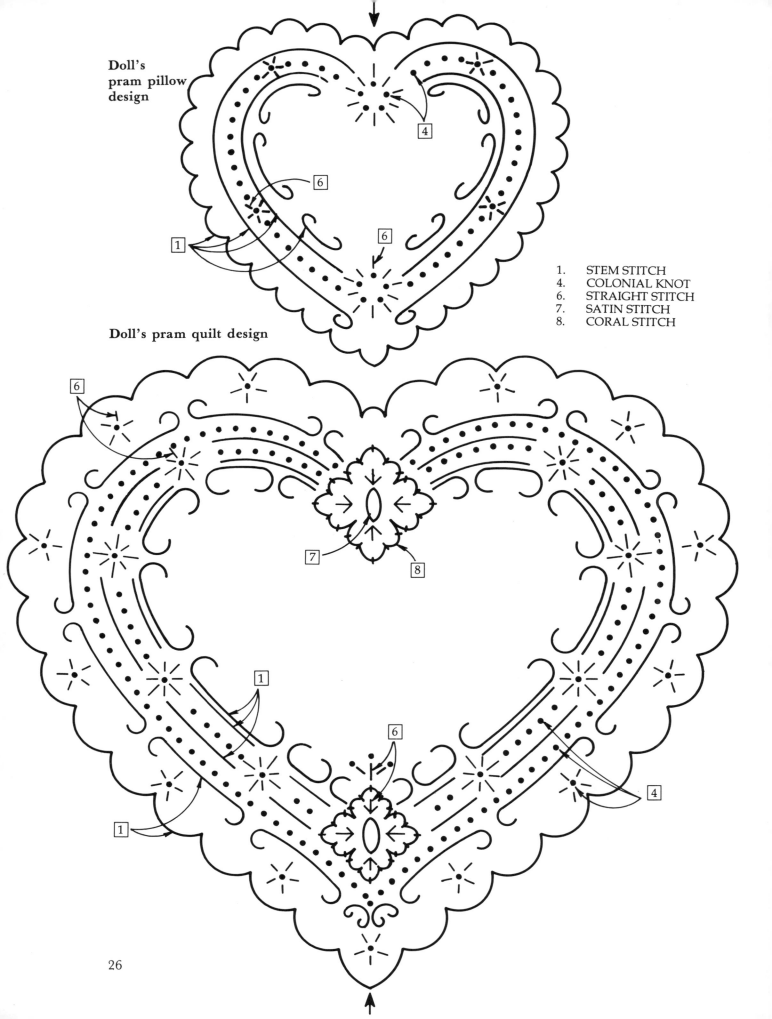

Doll's pram pillow design

Doll's pram quilt design

1. STEM STITCH
4. COLONIAL KNOT
6. STRAIGHT STITCH
7. SATIN STITCH
8. CORAL STITCH

26

Mini quilt and pillow pattern and design

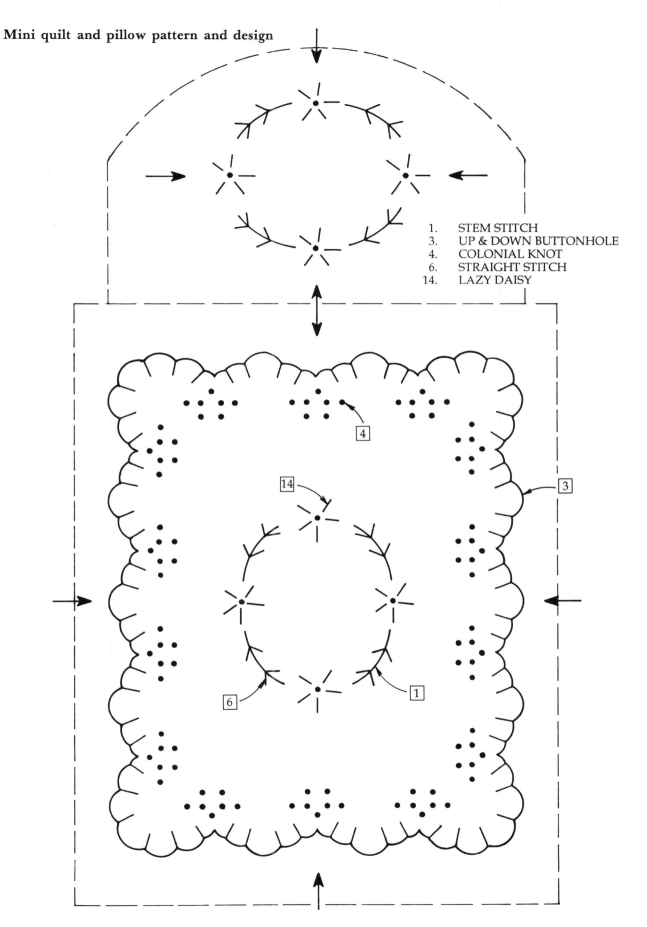

1. STEM STITCH
3. UP & DOWN BUTTONHOLE
4. COLONIAL KNOT
6. STRAIGHT STITCH
14. LAZY DAISY

Mini Quilt and Pillow

Illustrated on page 34

Materials

Note: Before cutting the fabric and lace wash following instructions on page 7.

calico or homespun for fronts and backs of quilt and pillow, 20 cm × 30 cm (8'' × 11¾'')
flat cotton lace, 1 m × 10 mm (39'' × ½'')
Pelon, 20 cm × 30 cm (8'' × 11¾'')
polyester stuffing
tracing paper

1. Trace the designs and patterns on page 27 onto tracing paper.
2. Transfer both back and front quilt and pillow patterns and designs from the tracing paper onto the right side of the fabric, following instructions on page 9. *Do not cut out.*
3. Tack the Pelon to the wrong side of the fabric. Place the fabric in a hoop and pull taut.
4. Work the candlewick embroidery on the front pieces.

5. When complete cut out the patterns. Wash out blue pen markings in cold water. Allow fabric to dry, then press carefully with a warm iron.
6. Pin and tack the lace, right sides and raw edges together, to the front of the quilt and pillow. Make sure extra gathering is added to corners to avoid pulled corners.
7. With right sides together, pin and tack the backings to the front quilt and pillow pieces. Stitch a 5 mm (¼'') seam around the edges, leaving a 7 cm (2¾'') opening in the centre of the base of both items for turning through.
8. Zigzag or overlock seams, clip corners and remove tacking. Turn right side out.
9. Fold the raw edges at the opening 5 mm (¼'') inside the quilt and pillow and press to create a neat seam. Neatly slip stitch opening closed on the quilt.
10. Remove all remaining tacking on the quilt and press carefully.
11. Remove all remaining tacking on the pillow. Fill opening carefully with stuffing. Neatly slip stitch the opening closed.

Muffin Rag Doll

Illustrated on page 35

Materials

Note: Before cutting the fabric and lace wash following instructions on page 7.

calico or homespun for head, arms and legs, 20 cm × 40 cm (7¾'' × 15¾'')
ribbon for hair, 15 cm × 5 mm (6'' × ¼'')
brown and pink embroidery cotton for eyes and mouth
satay skewer to make hair
tracing paper
polyester stuffing
cotton for hair, 2 m (2 yds)

1. Trace the design and patterns on the opposite page onto tracing paper.
2. Transfer the body front and back pattern and design from tracing paper onto the fabric, following the instructions on page 9. *Do not cut out.*
3. Place the fabric in the hoop and pull taut.
4. Work the candlewick embroidery on the front piece.

5. Once candlewicking is complete, cut out the outline of the bodies. Wash out blue pen markings with cold water. Allow the fabric to dry, then press with a warm iron.
6. Cut out the pieces for the head, arms and legs.
7. *Step-by step:* Clip all curved allowances for ease. Join all pieces together with right sides facing.
8. Sew leg sections together leaving top edges open. Turn right side out. Stuff firmly, leaving top edge clear for stitching.
9. Sew arms in same manner as legs.
10. With neck edges matching, sew head sections to body sections.
11. Flatten and pin legs so that seams are aligned. Position open ends of legs and arms to front of body as shown in Figure 1. Pin and stitch into place.
12. Pin and tack front and back body pieces together with finished arms and legs on inside of body pieces. Stitch a 5 mm (¼'') seam around the edges, leaving a 6 cm (2½'') opening in the centre of the bottom end of the doll for turning (Figure 2).
13. Remove tacking and turn right side out through opening.

Muffin rag doll pattern and deisgn

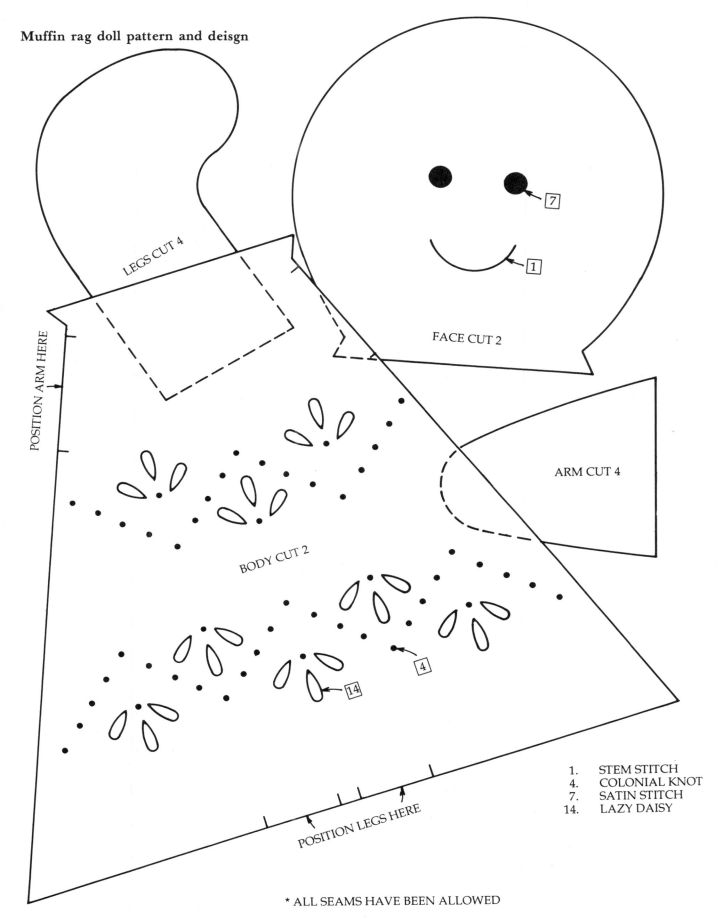

LEGS CUT 4

POSITION ARM HERE

FACE CUT 2

ARM CUT 4

BODY CUT 2

7

1

14

4

1. STEM STITCH
4. COLONIAL KNOT
7. SATIN STITCH
14. LAZY DAISY

POSITION LEGS HERE

* ALL SEAMS HAVE BEEN ALLOWED

14. Stuff firmly with polyester stuffing. Neatly stitch the opening closed.
15. Wet the cotton for the hair, wrap tightly around

skewer and dry in a moderate oven for 15 minutes.
16. Stitch hair on top of head. Tie a bow and stitch on top of hair.

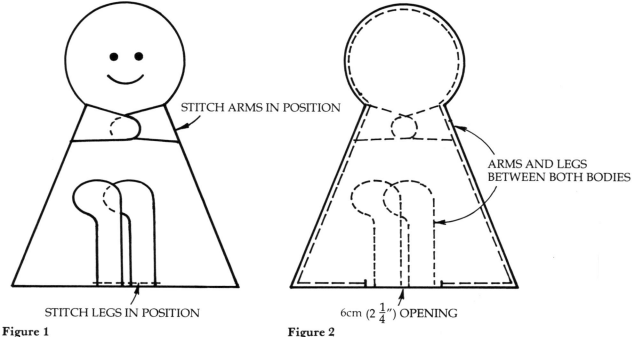

STITCH ARMS IN POSITION

STITCH LEGS IN POSITION

Figure 1

ARMS AND LEGS BETWEEN BOTH BODIES

6cm (2¼") OPENING

Figure 2

Illustrated on page 35

Cushion

Materials

Note: Before cutting fabric and lace wash following instructions on page 7.

calico or homespun for frill, 2 strips 1.20 m × 16.5 cm (1⅜ yd × 6½")
calico or homespun for cushion top and backing, 2 pieces 37 cm (14½") square
calico or homespun for zipper back, 2 pieces 37 cm × 19 cm (14½" × 7½")
apparel wadding, 37 cm (14½") square
35 cm (14") nylon zipper
No. 14 cushion insert
flat cotton lace, 2.50 m × 4 cm (2¾ yd × 1½")
tracing paper

1. Trace the design on the opposite page onto tracing paper.
2. Fold the fabric front piece in half horizontally and then vertically, pressing your fingernail across the folds to create crease marks. Match the arrows to the crease lines on your fabric. Pin the fabric front and pattern together.
3. Transfer the design from the tracing paper onto the front fabric piece, following the instructions on page 9. Tack the wadding to the wrong side of the front fabric. Place the fabric in a hoop and pull taut.
4. Work the candlewick embroidery on the front fabric piece.
5. When complete, wash out the blue pen markings with cold water. Allow the fabric to dry, then carefully press with a warm iron.
6. To complete the cushion follow the instructions on pages 16–17 for making a ruffle and cushion.

Cushion design

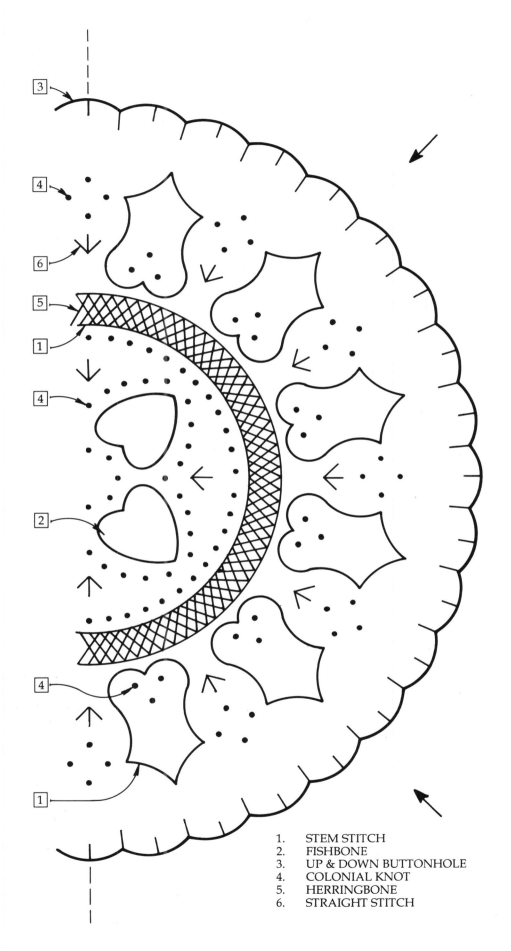

1. STEM STITCH
2. FISHBONE
3. UP & DOWN BUTTONHOLE
4. COLONIAL KNOT
5. HERRINGBONE
6. STRAIGHT STITCH

31

Round Table Cloth

Materials

Note: Before cutting the fabric and lace wash following instructions on page 7.

calico or homespun, circle 65 cm (25¼'') diameter
flat cotton lace, 2.50 m × 4 cm (90'' × 1½'')
tracing paper

1. Trace the design below onto tracing paper.
2. Fold the fabric circle into quarters following the diagrams for the scone warmer on page 86.
3. Following the instructions on page 9 transfer the design from the tracing paper onto the fabric in each quarter, matching the lines on the design with the crease lines on the fabric. Place the fabric in a hoop and pull taut.

**Design for
Round table cloth**
and
Oval table runner
(page 54)

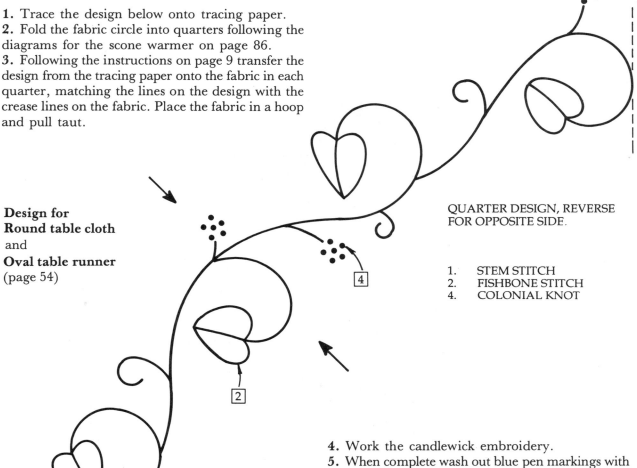

QUARTER DESIGN, REVERSE
FOR OPPOSITE SIDE.

1.   STEM STITCH
2.   FISHBONE STITCH
4.   COLONIAL KNOT

PLACE ON CREASE LINE

PLACE ON CREASE LINE

4. Work the candlewick embroidery.
5. When complete wash out blue pen markings with cold water. Allow the fabric to dry, then press carefully with a warm iron.
6. Make a hem around the circle by turning fabric under 5 mm (¼''), and pressing. Turn under 5 mm (¼'') again and press; pin, tack and machine stitch.
7. Sew the lace to the right side of the table cloth as near to the edge as possible, easing the lace so that it doesn't drag and pucker. Leave a few centimetres at each end for joining.
8. Join the ends of the lace with a French seam. Pin the lace wrong sides together and machine stitch a 5 mm (¼'') seam. Now turn the lace, placing right sides together, and stitch a slightly wider seam than before. Ease and machine stitch to the fabric.

THE FAMILY ROOM

A charming collection of treasures old and new

Wall hanging (page 20)

Left: *Doll's pram quilt and pillow (page 24)*

Below: *Mini quilt and pillow (page 28)*

Left: *Muffin rag doll (page 28)*

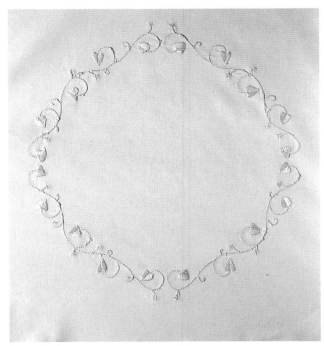

Round table cloth (page 32)

Family room cushion (page 30)

THE LOUNGE ROOM

Candlewicked items add to the warmth of the room

Framed picture (page 48)

Right: *Double wedding ring cushion (page 46)*

Oval table runner (page 46)

Antimacassar set in lounge rom setting (page 42)
Below: *Detail of antimacassar, pincushion and scissor holder*

THE SEWING ROOM

Candlewicked items add to the pleasure of working in this room

Sewing machine table cover (page 52)

Sewing organiser (page 53)

40

THE LOUNGE ROOM

Antimacassars

The materials and instructions specified here will allow you to make sufficient pieces for a two-seater settee and two armchairs. This design allows for the pincushion and scissor holder to be removed from the antimacassar when not being used.

Antimacassar design

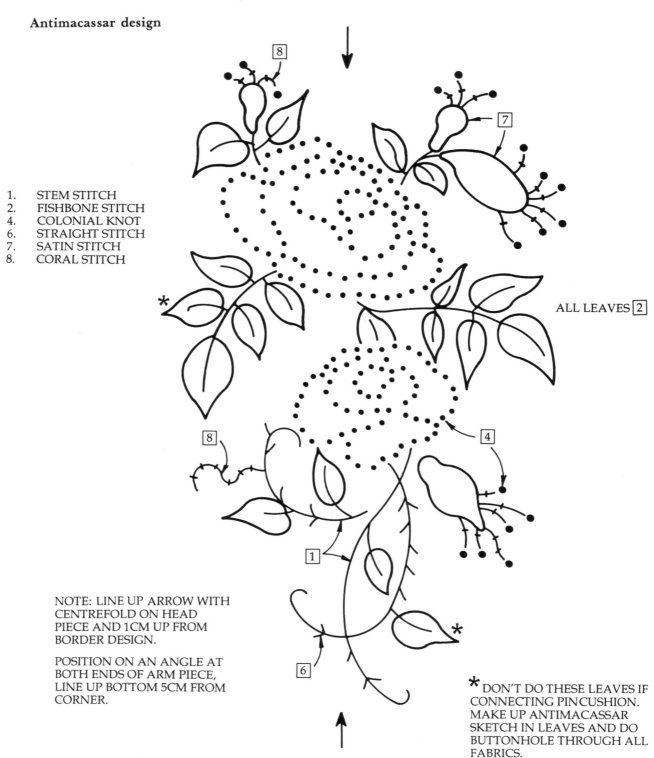

1. STEM STITCH
2. FISHBONE STITCH
4. COLONIAL KNOT
6. STRAIGHT STITCH
7. SATIN STITCH
8. CORAL STITCH

ALL LEAVES 2

NOTE: LINE UP ARROW WITH CENTREFOLD ON HEAD PIECE AND 1CM UP FROM BORDER DESIGN.

POSITION ON AN ANGLE AT BOTH ENDS OF ARM PIECE, LINE UP BOTTOM 5CM FROM CORNER.

* DON'T DO THESE LEAVES IF CONNECTING PINCUSHION. MAKE UP ANTIMACASSAR SKETCH IN LEAVES AND DO BUTTONHOLE THROUGH ALL FABRICS.

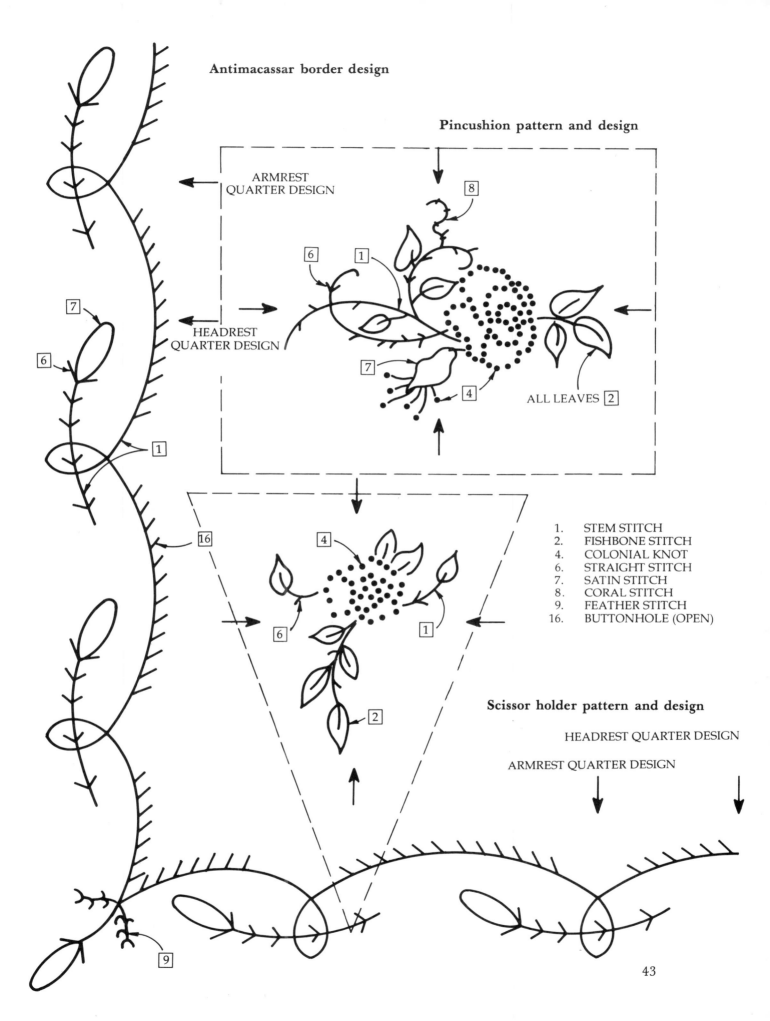

Antimacassar border design

Pincushion pattern and design

ARMREST
QUARTER DESIGN

8

6 1

7

HEADREST
QUARTER DESIGN

7

6

1

4

ALL LEAVES 2

16

4

6

1

2

1.   STEM STITCH
2.   FISHBONE STITCH
4.   COLONIAL KNOT
6.   STRAIGHT STITCH
7.   SATIN STITCH
8.   CORAL STITCH
9.   FEATHER STITCH
16.   BUTTONHOLE (OPEN)

Scissor holder pattern and design

HEADREST QUARTER DESIGN

ARMREST QUARTER DESIGN

9

43

Note: Before cutting the fabric and lace wash following instructions on page 7.

satin ribbon for connecting pincushion, 2 lengths 10 mm × 15 cm (½'' × 6'')
Pelon, 90 cm × 3 m (1 yd × 3½ yds)
calico or homespun, 115 cm × 4 m (1¼ yds × 4⅜ yds)
flat cotton lace, 15 m × 25 mm (16½ yds × 1'')
tracing paper

1. Trace the designs on pages 50–51 onto tracing paper.
2. Cut two pieces of fabric, each 43 cm × 90 cm (16¾'' × 1 yd) for front and back of the two-seater headrest covers, four 43 cm (16¾'') squares for the fronts and backs of the two single headrest covers, twelve pieces of fabric 35 cm × 51 cm (13½'' × 20'') for the fronts and backs of the six armrest covers. Cut two pieces of Pelon 43 cm (16¾'') square and six pieces 35 cm × 51 cm (13½'' × 20'').
3. Transfer the designs from the tracing paper onto the front fabric pieces following the instructions on page 9. Tack the Pelon to the wrong side of all the front pieces except the largest one. Place a front piece in the hoop and pull fabric taut.
4. Work the candlewick embroidery on all front pieces. If you choose to connect the pincushion and scissor holder to one of the armrests, omit the leaves with the asterisks from the design.
5. When complete wash out blue pen markings with cold water. Allow the fabric to dry, then carefully press with a warm iron.
6. Pin the lace, right sides and raw edges together, to the front pieces, making sure that you allow extra fullness at the corners. Machine stitch the lace in place, 3 mm (⅛'') from the edge.
7. Place the backing pieces and the fronts together with right sides facing. Pin and tack the layers together and stitch around all four sides, leaving a 15 cm (5¾'') opening on one side. Zigzag around the raw edges or overlock, then remove the tacking thread. Turn the antimacassar to the right side through the opening.
8. Neatly slip stitch the opening closed.
9. To connect the pincushion to the armrest: Freehand sketch the leaves with asterisks on, using the water-soluble pen. Embroider with buttonhole stitch through all layers of fabric. Carefully slit the buttonholes. Slip stitch the ribbons to the back of the antimacassar close to the buttonholes. Pull the ribbons through the buttonholes. (The ribbons can be pulled to the back when the pincushion is not in use.)

Pincushion and Scissor Holder

Materials

Note: Before cutting the fabric and lace wash following instructions on page 7.

calico or homespun for pincushion and scissor holder, 15 cm × 70 cm (6'' × 27½'')
flat cotton lace for pincushion, 40 cm × 25 mm (15¾'' × 1'')
insertion lace for scissor holder, 10 mm × 60 cm (½'' × 23½'')
polyester stuffing
Pelon for scissor holder, 30 cm (11¾'') square
tracing paper
satin ribbon for pincushion, 2 lengths 10 mm × 15 cm (½'' × 6'')
satin ribbon for scissor holder, 5 mm × 9 cm (¼'' × 3½'')

1. Trace designs and patterns on page 51 onto tracing paper.
2. Transfer the pincushion pattern twice and the scissor holder pattern four times onto the fabric, then transfer the designs onto the front pattern pieces only, following the instructions on page 9. *Do not cut out.*
3. Place a fabric piece in the hoop and pull taut. Work the candlewick embroidery on all front pieces.
4. When complete, cut the patterns out and wash out the blue pen markings in cold water. Allow the fabric to dry, then carefully press with a warm iron.

Pincushion
1. Pin and tack the lace, right sides and raw edges together, to the front of the pincushion. Make sure extra gathering is added to corners to avoid pulled corners. Position ribbons right sides together in the centres of the narrow ends (Figure 1).
2. Pin and tack the back to the front of the pincushion with right sides together. Stitch a 5 mm (¼'') opening on one side (Figure 1) for turning through.
3. Zigzag or overlock seams, clip corners and remove tacking. Turn right side out.
4. Fold the raw edges at the opening 5 mm (¼'') inside the pincushion and press to create a neat seam. Fill with polyester stuffing. Neatly slip stitch the opening closed.

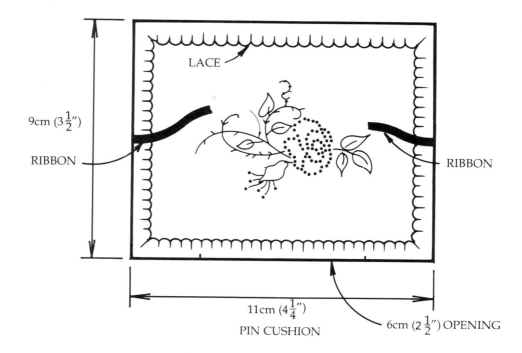

Figure 1

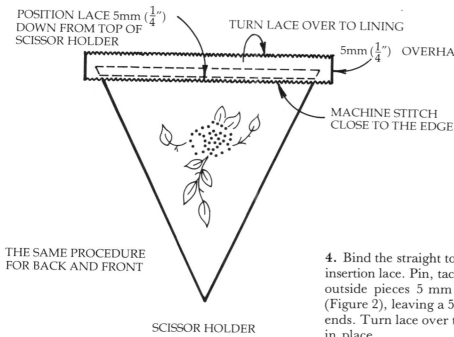

Figure 2

Scissor Holder

1. Four pieces of fabric make up the scissor holder—1 back, 2 linings and 1 candlewicked top.

2. Cut 2 pieces of Pelon to the shape of the scissor holder pattern on page 51.

3. Pin and tack Pelon pieces between front fabric and lining and back fabric and lining.

4. Bind the straight top edge of front and back with insertion lace. Pin, tack and stitch the lace onto both outside pieces 5 mm (¼'') down from top edge (Figure 2), leaving a 5 mm (¼'') overhang on both ends. Turn lace over to lining and neatly slip stitch in place.

5. Place back and top linings together, pin and tack.

6. Bind the sides of scissor holder, starting at the top right hand side and allowing a 10 mm (½'') overlap at the top. Pin, tack and stitch the lace 5 mm (¼'') in from edge, turn overlap down over top edge, turn lace over to back of scissor holder and neatly slip stitch in place. Repeat the same for the left hand side with a 10 mm (½'') overlap both ends.

7. Fold ribbon in half and neatly stitch in centre of back.

Illustrated on page 37

Oval Table Runner

Materials

Note: Before cutting the fabric and lace wash following instructions on page 7.

calico or homespun, oval 51 cm × 32 cm (20'' × 12½'')
flat lace, 1.80 m × 6 cm (70½'' × 2½'')
tracing paper

1. Trace the border design on page 32 onto tracing paper.
2. Fold the fabric oval in half horizontally and then vertically. Press your fingernail across the folds to create crease marks. Match the crease line marks on the pattern with the crease lines on the fabric. Pin the fabric and pattern together.
3. Transfer the design from the tracing paper onto the front fabric, matching the lines on the design with the crease lines on the fabric. Follow the instructions on page 9.
4. Work the candlewick embroidery on the front fabric piece.
5. When complete, wash out blue pen markings with cold water. Allow the fabric to dry, then press with a warm iron.
6. Make a hem on the edge of the oval by turning under 5 mm (¼'') and pressing. Turn under 5 mm (¼'') again and press; pin, tack and machine stitch.
7. Sew the lace to the right side of the table cloth as near to the edge as possible, easing the lace so that it doesn't drag and pucker. Leave a few centimetres free at each end for joining.
8. Join the lace by making a French seam. Pin the lace wrong sides together and machine stitch a 5 mm (¼'') seam; now turn the lace, place right sides together and stitch a slightly wider seam than before. Ease and machine stitch the lace to the fabric.

Illustrated on page 37

Double Wedding Ring Cushion

Materials

Note: Before cutting fabric wash following instructions on page 7

35 cm (14'') nylon zipper
calico or homespun for front and lining, 2 pieces 38 cm (14¾'') square
calico or homespun for backing, 2 pieces 21 cm × 38 cm (8'' × 14¾'')
apparel wadding, 38 cm (14¾'') square
calico or homespun for binding, 55 mm × 1.65 m (2'' × 1⅞ yds)
tracing paper
cream quilting cotton
quilting needles

1. Fold one fabric front piece in half horizontally and then vertically, pressing your fingernail across the folds to create crease marks.
2. Fold tracing paper in the same manner as fabric and draw faint lines on the creases to the paper. Place the paper over the design on page 9, matching arrows, and trace onto the paper.

Note: The drawing on the next page only shows one quarter of the cushion design, so you will need to turn your paper and trace in four sections.
3. Transfer the design from the tracing paper onto the front fabric piece, following instructions on page 9. Tack the wadding to the wrong side of the front piece. Place the front piece in the hoop and pull taut.
4. Work the candlewick embroidery on the front piece. *Note:* Only do the embroidery stitches at this point, leaving the broken lines for quilting.
5. Place lining and front wrong sides together, pin and tack.
6. The quilting can be done by sewing machine, following the broken lines on the design. If you do not wish to use the sewing machine, you can use hand stitches.
7. Hand quilting uses a simple running stitch. Use a hoop if you prefer. The stitches should be small, even and straight. Don't panic if your stitches look larger than you think they should; they will become smaller as you become more proficient.

To begin, tie a single knot in the end of a 40 cm (15½'') length of quilting thread. Begin quilting in the centre of the cushion, working to the outside.

Double wedding ring cushion design

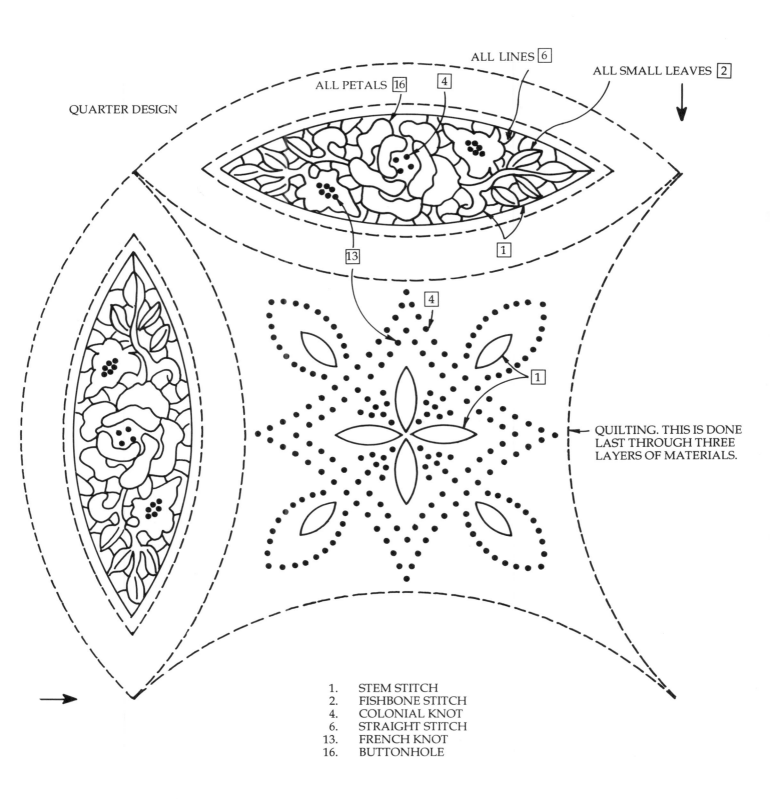

QUARTER DESIGN

ALL PETALS [16]

ALL LINES [6]

ALL SMALL LEAVES [2]

[4]

[13]

[1]

[4]

[1]

QUILTING. THIS IS DONE
LAST THROUGH THREE
LAYERS OF MATERIALS.

1.	STEM STITCH
2.	FISHBONE STITCH
4.	COLONIAL KNOT
6.	STRAIGHT STITCH
13.	FRENCH KNOT
16.	BUTTONHOLE

Insert the needle about 10 mm (⅛'') from the starting point. Tug gently on the thread until the knot pops through the fabric and is buried in the wadding. Take a backstitch then begin quilting, making a small running stitch that goes through all three layers. Continue with a gentle rocking motion, picking up two or three stitches at a time; try to keep them straight and even.

To finish off, tie a knot in the thread close to the last stitch. Take one more backstitch in your cushion, tugging the knot into the wadding layer. Bring the needle out a short distance away from your stitches, cut the thread close to the surface and let the end disappear into the cushion.

8. When complete, wash out blue pen markings in cold water, allow to dry, then carefully press with a warm iron.

9. Stitch the ends of the cushion back pieces together using a 1 cm (⅜'') seam for 10 mm (½''), and leaving an opening for the zipper (Figure 7, page 00). Press the seam open. Sew the zipper in place and open it.

10. With wrong sides together, pin and tack the front to the backing.

11. Fold the binding strip in half lengthwise, wrong sides together and raw edges matching. Press the binding.

12. Pin the binding, right sides and raw edges together, to the front piece. Turn the pressed edge of the binding to the back of the cushion, tack in position. Hand sew the binding in place using a neat slip stitch. Remove tacking.

Illustrated on page 37

Framed Picture

Materials

Note: Before cutting fabric wash following instructions on page 7.

frame of your choice
calico or homespun 5 cm (2'') larger than the outside measurements of the frame
apparel wadding the same size as the outside measurements of the frame
embroidery cotton (my choice, DMC Perlé No. 8)
tracing paper

1. Trace the design on the opposite page onto tracing paper.
2. Fold the fabric in half horizontally and then vertically, pressing your fingernail across the folds to create crease marks. Match the arrows on the pattern with the crease lines on the fabric. Pin the fabric and pattern together.
3. Transfer the design from the tracing paper onto the front fabric piece, following the instructions on page 9. Place fabric in hoop and pull taut.
4. Work the candlewick embroidery on the front fabric piece.
5. When complete wash out the blue pen markings with cold water. Allow fabric to dry, then press carefully with a warm iron.
6. Cut the fabric and wadding to the same size as the backing supplied with the frame, making sure you centre the design.
7. Glue the wadding to the backing. Place wrong side of fabric on top of wadding and set picture into frame.

Framed picture design

ALL THE SAME STITCHES
AS LARGER BASKET

Teapot cosy design
(page 84)

1.   STEM STITCH
2.   FISHBONE STITCH
4.   COLONIAL KNOT
6.   STRAIGHT STITCH
7.   SATIN STITCH
10. FLY STITCH
12. CHAIN STITCH
14. LAZY DAISY

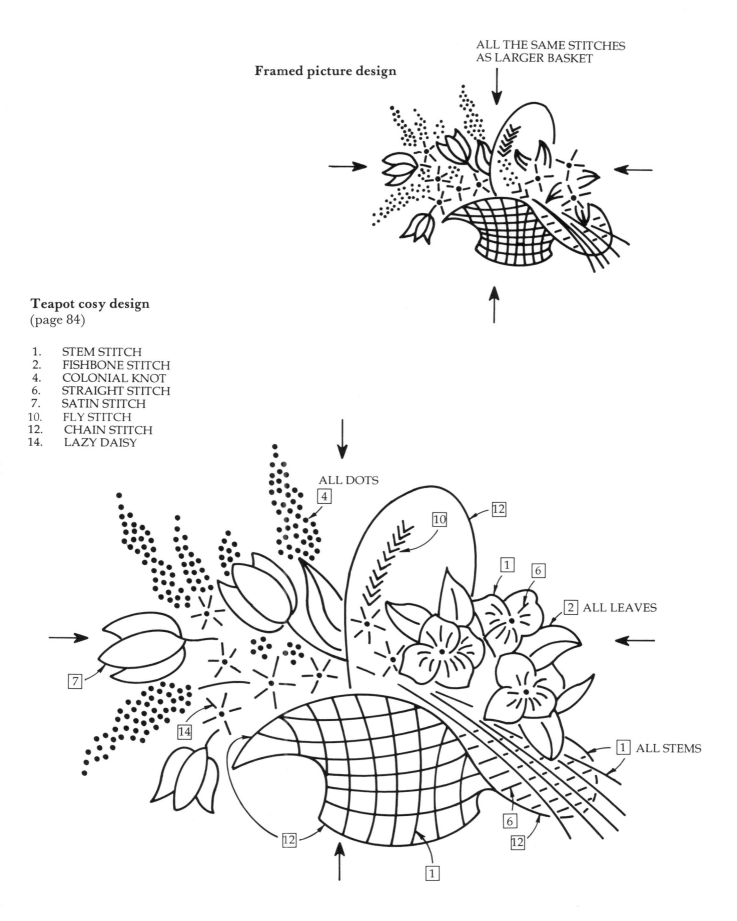

ALL DOTS
4

10   12

1   6

2 ALL LEAVES

7

14

1 ALL STEMS

12

1

6

12

49

THE SEWING ROOM

Sewing Machine Table Cover

Materials

Note: Before cutting the fabric and lace wash following instructions on page 7.

calico or homespun, 50 cm × 80 cm (19½'' × 31½'')
flat cotton lace, 2 pieces 60 cm × 6 cm (23½'' × 2¼'')
tracing paper

1. Trace the design below onto tracing paper.
2. Fold the fabric in half vertically so that it measures 80 cm × 25 cm (31½'' × 9¾''). Press with your fingernail across the fold to create a crease line. Match the vertical arrows on the pattern to the

Design for
Sewing machine table cover
and
Pillow cases
(page 73)

1. STEM STITCH
2. FISHBONE STITCH
4. COLONIAL KNOT
7. SATIN STITCH
14. LAZY DAISY

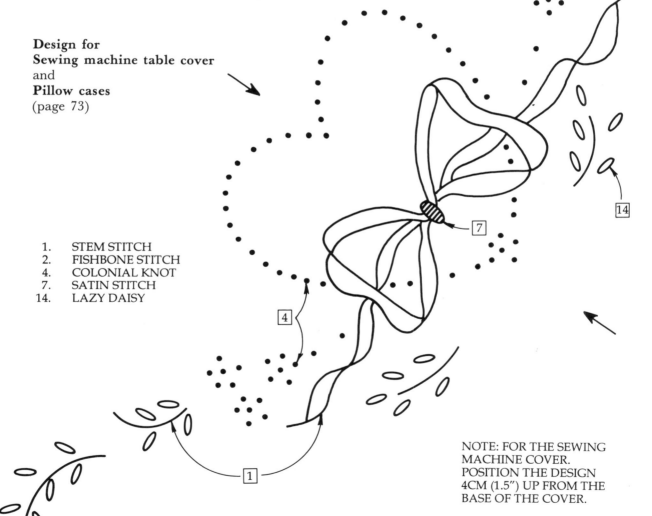

NOTE: FOR THE SEWING MACHINE COVER. POSITION THE DESIGN 4CM (1.5") UP FROM THE BASE OF THE COVER.

crease line. Position the design 4 cm (1½'') in from one short edge of the cover; pin the fabric and pattern together.

3. Transfer the design from the tracing paper onto the front fabric, following the instructions on page 9. Place the fabric into a hoop and pull taut.

4. Work the candlewick embroidery.

5. When complete, wash out blue pen markings with cold water. Allow the fabric to dry then carefully press with a warm iron.

6. Machine stitch a mitred hem around all four sides following instructions on page 15.

7. Stitch cotton lace to both short ends of the machine cover. Remember to make a narrow hem on both short ends of the lace.

Sewing Organiser, Chatelaine and Pincushion

Illustrated on page 53 and 57

Materials

Note: Before cutting fabric and lace wash following instructions on page 7.

calico or homespun, 80 cm × 40 cm (31¼'' × 15½'')
gathered cotton lace for organiser and pincushion, 1 m × 20 mm (39'' × ⅝'')
flat cotton lace for chatelaine, 1.80 m × 10 mm (2 yds × ½'')
satin ribbon for organiser and chatelaine, 1 m × 5 mm (39'' × ¼'')
Pelon for organiser, 23 cm × 16 cm (9'' × 6'')

plastic press stud
tracing paper
polyester stuffing for pincushion and heart

Note: The organiser, chatelaine and pincushion should be worked on the same piece of fabric. Should you wish to make only one of the items the piece of fabric you are working on must be large enough to fit into a hoop.

1. Trace the designs on pages 54–56 onto the tracing paper. Use the border from the wall hanging (page 22) for the chatelaine belt.

2. On the right side of the fabric mark out the pieces

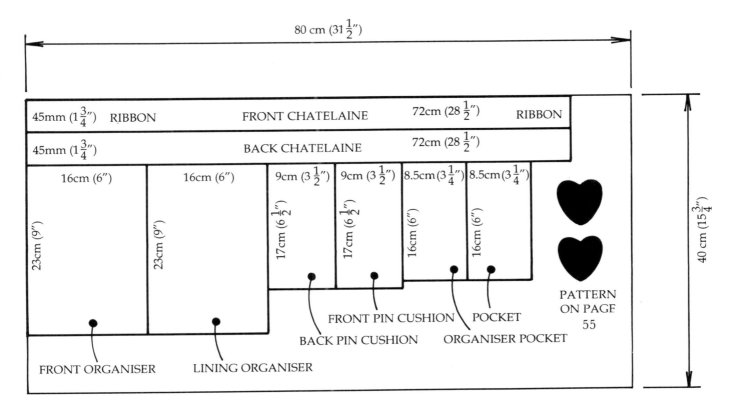

Sewing organiser design

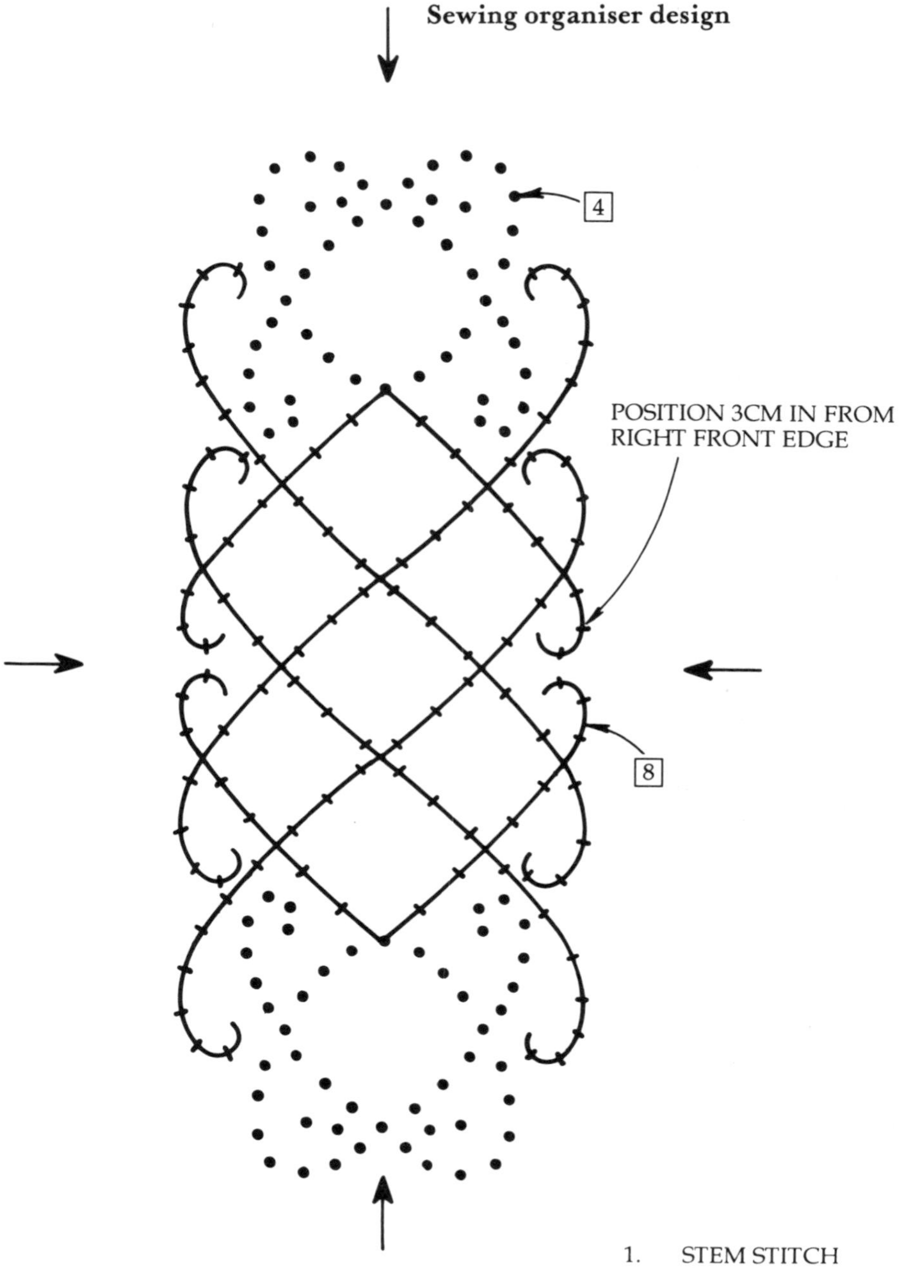

4

POSITION 3CM IN FROM
RIGHT FRONT EDGE

8

1. STEM STITCH
4. COLONIAL KNOT
8. CORAL STITCH
13. FRENCH KNOT

as shown in the cutting diagram; seams have been allowed. Transfer the designs onto the right side of the front pieces. The organiser design includes instructions for positioning it. The pincushion design has arrows to centre the design on the pattern piece. The chatelaine heart design is included on the pattern piece. Do not cut out the individual pattern pieces; they are too small to fit in a hoop for candlewicking.

3. Work the candlewick embroidery on the front fabric pieces.

4. When embroidery is complete cut out the individual pieces. Wash out the blue pen markings with cold water. Allow the fabric to dry, then press with a warm iron.

Sewing organiser

1. Zigzag or overlock one long side of pockets. With wrong sides together turn a 10 mm (½'') hem on these overlocked sides, press and machine stitch.

2. Centre 13 cm (5'') of satin ribbon on both 16 cm (6'') ends of the front of the sewing organiser.

3. Pin, tack and machine stitch the gathered lace to the right side and raw edges of the 23 cm (9'') edge of the front of the sewing organiser.

4. With right sides and raw edges together, pin and tack the pockets to both short ends of the front of the organiser. Pin lining and front fabric right sides together. Place Pelon on top of lining. Pin, tack and machine stitch a 5 mm (¼'') seam, leaving a 9 cm (3½'') opening in the centre of one long side of the organiser for turning through.

5. Zigzag or overlock seams. Clip the corners. Remove the tacking and turn right side out.

6. Carefully slip stitch the opening closed.

Chatelaine

1. Pin and tack the 10 mm (½'') lace, right sides and raw edges together, to the long sides of the chatelaine.

2. Pin and tack the lining to the front of the chatelaine with right sides together. Stitch a 5 mm

(¼'') seam around the edges, leaving a 9 cm (3½'') opening in the centre of one long side for turning through.

3. Zigzag or overlock seams, clip corners and remove tacking. Turn right side out.

4. Fold the raw edges at the opening 5 mm (¼'') inside the chatelaine and press to create a neat 5 mm (¼'') seam. Slip stitch closed.

5. Neatly slip stitch 10 cm (3¾'') of satin ribbon to both ends of the chatelaine. Stitch a press stud on the back right-hand side of the chatelaine and to the end of the ribbon on the same side.

Heart for chatelaine

1. Pin and tack the 10 mm (½'') lace, right sides and raw edges together, to the front of the heart. Make sure extra gather is added to the corners to avoid pulled corners.

2. Pin and tack the backing to the front of the heart with right sides together. Stitch a 5 mm (¼'') seam around the edges leaving a 4 cm (1½'') opening on one side for turning through.

3. Clip the curves, remove the tacking and turn right side out.

4. Fill the heart with polyester stuffing and slip stitch the opening closed.

5. Neatly slip stitch the satin ribbon connected to the chatelaine to the heart.

Chatelaine heart pattern and design

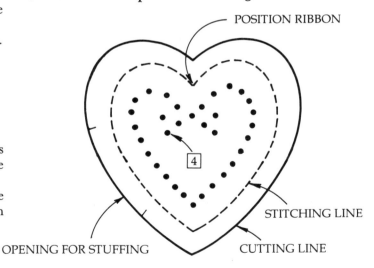

POSITION RIBBON

STITCHING LINE

CUTTING LINE

OPENING FOR STUFFING

Pincushion

1. Pin and tack the lace, right sides and raw edges together, to the front of the pincushion. Make sure extra gather is added to the corners to avoid pulled corners.

2. Pin and tack the back of the pincushion to the front with right sides together. Stitch a 5 mm (¼") seam around the edges, leaving a 6 cm (2¼") opening on one long side for turning through.

3. Zigzag or overlock seams, clip the corners and remove tacking. Turn right side out.

4. Fold the raw edges at the opening 5 mm (¼") inside the pincushion and press to create a neat 5 mm (¼") seam. Fill with polyester stuffing. Neatly slip stitch the opening closed.

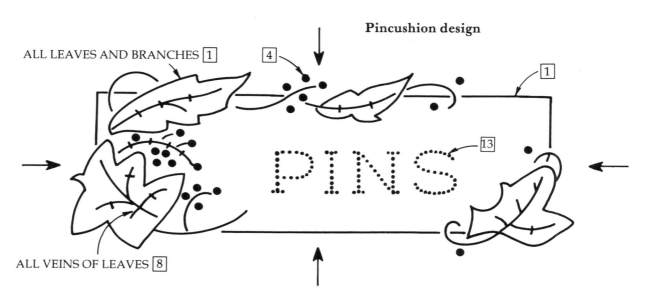

Pincushion design

ALL LEAVES AND BRANCHES [1]

ALL VEINS OF LEAVES [8]

1. STEM STITCH
4. COLONIAL KNOT
8. CORAL STITCH
13. FRENCH KNOT

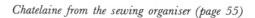

Chatelaine from the sewing organiser (page 55)

Pincushion from the sewing organiser (opposite page)

THE BEDROOM

Candlewicking brings a feminine touch

Initial brooch (page 66)

Right: *Brooch cushion (page 66)*

Pillow cases (page 73)

Coathanger (page 78)

Left: *Dress for porcelain doll (page 74)*

Opposite page: *Summer dress and nightie (page 71)*

Below: *Nightie bag (page 68)*

THE GARDEN

Old-world touches amongst the greenery

Rose pruning gloves (page 82)

Table cloth (page 82)

Teapot cosy (page 84)
Scone warmer (page 85)

THE BEDROOM

Brooch

Illustrated on page 59

Materials

This attractive 'initial brooch' is made with a Framecraft brooch base, which is available from most needlework and craft shops.

Working with a fine fabric is recommended. Mounting heavier fabrics is very difficult.

silk fabric (large enough to fit in a small quilting frame)
iron-on Vilene a little larger than the brooch frame (the Vilene prevents the fabric wrinkling when mounted)
Kanagawa silk thread
tracing paper
pencil (the water-soluble pen tends to 'bleed' on silk)

1. Trace the design from the opposite page onto tracing paper, selecting the initial of your choice to go into the centre of the design.
2. Carefully transfer the design from the tracing paper onto the silk fabric with a pencil, following the instructions on page 9.
3. Iron the Vilene onto the back of the fabric behind the design. Place fabric in a small hoop and pull taut.
4. Candlewick the design, using one strand for the initial, two strands for the bow and the whole strand for knots and feather stitch.
5. When complete, press carefully with a warm iron.
6. Follow the manufacturer's instructions for cutting out and framing.

Brooch Cushion

Illustrated on page 59

Materials

Note: Before cutting the fabric and lace wash following instructions on page 7.

calico or homespun for back and front, 2 pieces 16 cm (6¼'') square
apparel wadding for top backing, 16 cm (6¼'') square
gathered lace, 80 cm × 3 cm (31½'' × 1¼'')
tracing paper
polyester stuffing

1. Trace the design on the opposite page onto the tracing paper.
2. Transfer the design from the tracing paper onto the fabric front, following the instructions on page 9.
3. Pin and tack the wadding to the wrong side of the front fabric. Place in a hoop and pull taut.
4. Work the candlewick embroidery on the front piece.

5. When complete wash out blue pen markings with cold water. Allow the fabric to dry then carefully press with a warm iron.
6. Pin and tack the lace, right sides and raw edges together, to.the front of the brooch cushion, making sure extra gather is added to corners to avoid pulled corners.
7. With right sides together, pin and tack the back to the front of the cushion. Stitch a 5 mm (¼'') seam around the edges, leaving a 7 cm (2¾'') opening in the centre of one side for turning through.
8. Zigzag or overlock seams, clip the corners and remove tacking. Turn right side out.
9. Fold the raw edges at the opening 5 mm (¼'') inside the brooch cushion and press to create a neat seam. Neatly slip stitch opening closed.
10. Remove all remaining tacking on the cushion, fill carefully with stuffing then neatly slip stitch the opening closed.

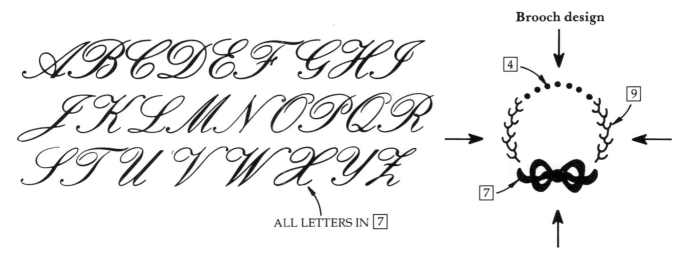

Brooch design

ALL LETTERS IN 7

4. COLONIAL KNOT
7. SATIN STITCH
9. FEATHER STITCH

Brooch cushion design

Illustrated on page 61

Nightie Bag

Materials

Note: Before cutting the fabric and lace wash following instructions on page 7.

calico or homespun for front and lining, 39 cm × 1.68 m (15¼'' × 65½'')
Pelon, 39 cm × 26 cm (15¼'' × 10¼'')
tracing paper, 45 cm × 26 cm (17½'' × 10¼'')

1. Fold the tracing paper in half vertically and trace the nightie bag design on the opposite page, tracing the left-hand side first and then the right. Then trace the border design from page 70 in position, following the instructions.

2. Fold the fabric in half vertically so that it measures 84 cm × 39 cm (32¾'' × 15¼'') wide. Press your fingernail across the fold to create a creased mark. Draw a vertical line on this creased mark, which will become the base line of the nightie bag (Figure 1).

3. Fold the fabric in half vertically so that it measures 19 cm × 84 cm (7¼'' × 32¾'') wide, and press the fold.

4. Transfer the designs from the tracing paper onto the front fabric piece, positioning the edges of the design on the tracing paper 12 mm (⅞'') from the base line (Figure 1). *Do not cut out,* as it would be very difficult to candlewick on the edge.

5. Tack the Pelon to the wrong side of the front fabric piece, on the base line. Place the front piece in the hoop and pull the fabric taut.

6. Work the candlewick embroidery on the front piece.

7. When you have completed the candlewicking mark 22 mm (⅞'') from the design to the base line, following the shape of the scallop. Fold the lining on the base line to the wrong side of the front fabric. Cut both fabrics out to the new scalloped shape (Figure 1).

8. Wash out the blue pen markings in cold water. Allow the fabric to dry, then press with a warm iron.

9. With right sides together pin, tack and machine stitch the front fabric to the lining fabric along the scalloped and straight edges. Clip the curves on the scalloped edge.

10. Turn through to the right side and carefully press the seams.

11. Turn it back to the wrong side so that the right sides are together. Turn the straight edge into the centre of the nightie bag 25 cm (9½'') (Figure 2). Pin and tack.

12. Stitch down both sides, leaving a 12 cm (4¾'') opening on one side for turning through.

13. Remove the tacking and turn the nightie bag right side out. Neatly slip stitch the opening closed.

14. Fold the flap over to the front 27 cm (10½'') and press the fold.

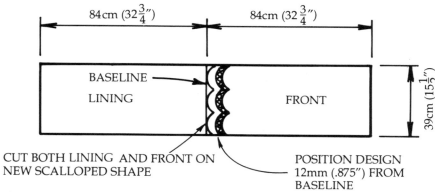

Figure 1

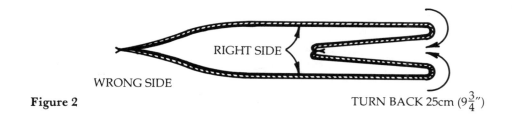

Figure 2

Nightie bag design

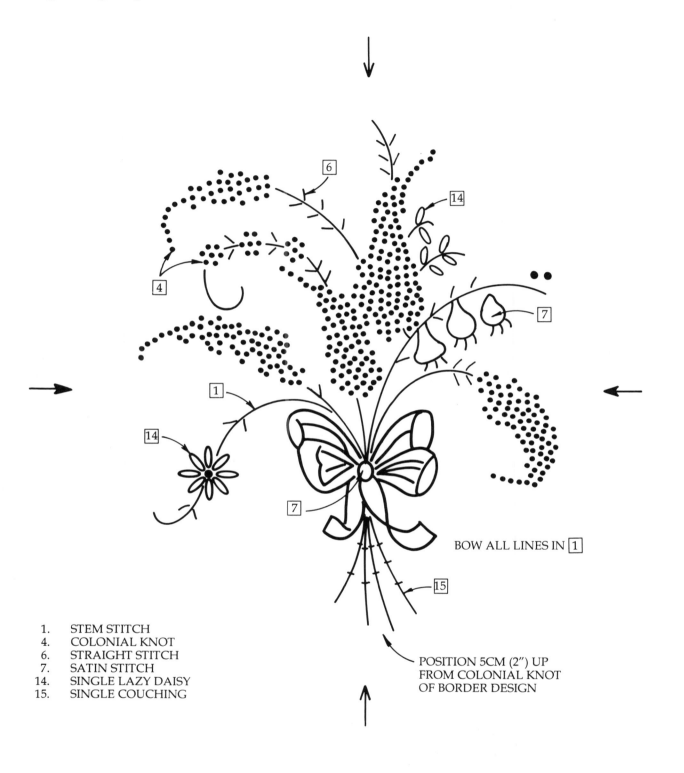

BOW ALL LINES IN [1]

POSITION 5CM (2") UP
FROM COLONIAL KNOT
OF BORDER DESIGN

1. STEM STITCH
4. COLONIAL KNOT
6. STRAIGHT STITCH
7. SATIN STITCH
14. SINGLE LAZY DAISY
15. SINGLE COUCHING

Nightie bag border design

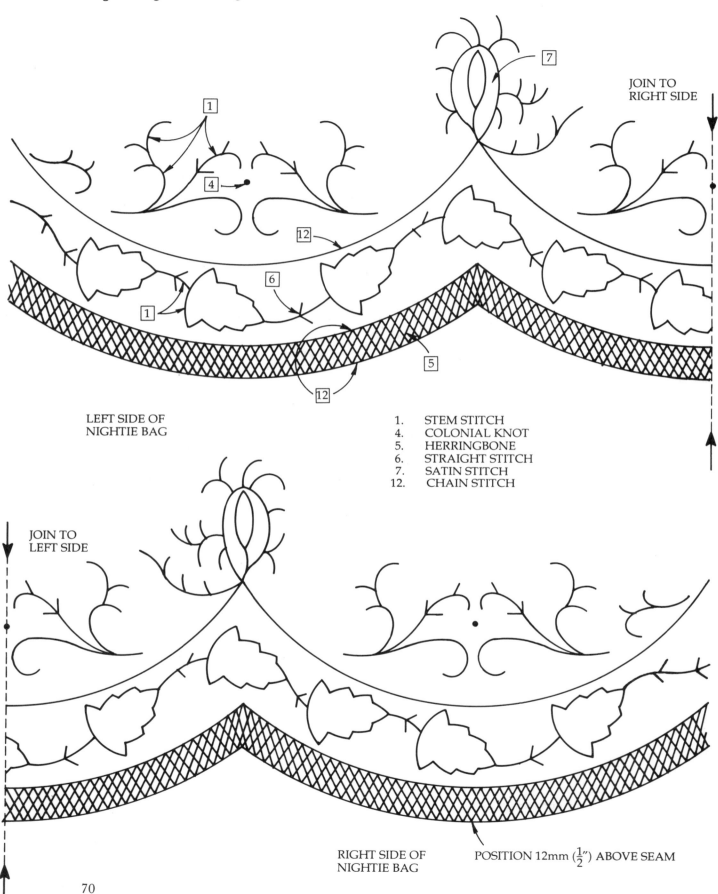

JOIN TO
RIGHT SIDE

LEFT SIDE OF
NIGHTIE BAG

1.   STEM STITCH
4.   COLONIAL KNOT
5.   HERRINGBONE
6.   STRAIGHT STITCH
7.   SATIN STITCH
12. CHAIN STITCH

JOIN TO
LEFT SIDE

RIGHT SIDE OF
NIGHTIE BAG

POSITION 12mm ($\frac{1}{2}$″) ABOVE SEAM

Illustrated on page 60 # Nightie and Summer Dress

Delicate candlewick embroidery enhances clothing. It can change the whole appearance of a garment, giving it that finishing feminine touch.

There are no restrictions on where one can use candlewicking, as you can see in the picture on page 60. The dress has embroidery on the tips of the collar and in a wide panel down the front. I have added a special touch to the nightie by embroidering the yoke, giving both garments an old-world appearance. I hope these garments will inspire readers to give their individual touches to what might otherwise be fairly basic garments.

Candlewick embroidery can be worked on a large range of clothing, including jackets, pockets, children's garments, baby clothing, doll's clothes and blouses.

The designs for the embroidery for the dress and the nightie are both included in this book; the nightie on this page, the dress on page 72.

Nightie design

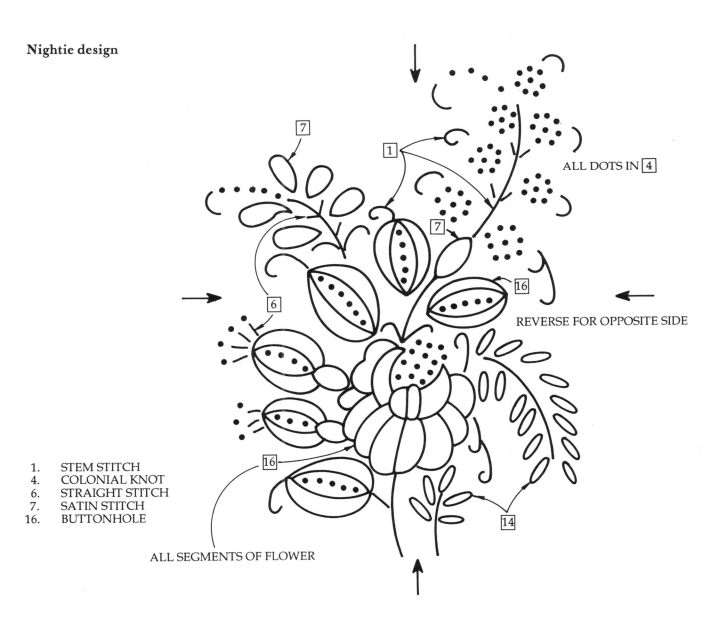

ALL DOTS IN 4

REVERSE FOR OPPOSITE SIDE

1. STEM STITCH
4. COLONIAL KNOT
6. STRAIGHT STITCH
7. SATIN STITCH
16. BUTTONHOLE

ALL SEGMENTS OF FLOWER

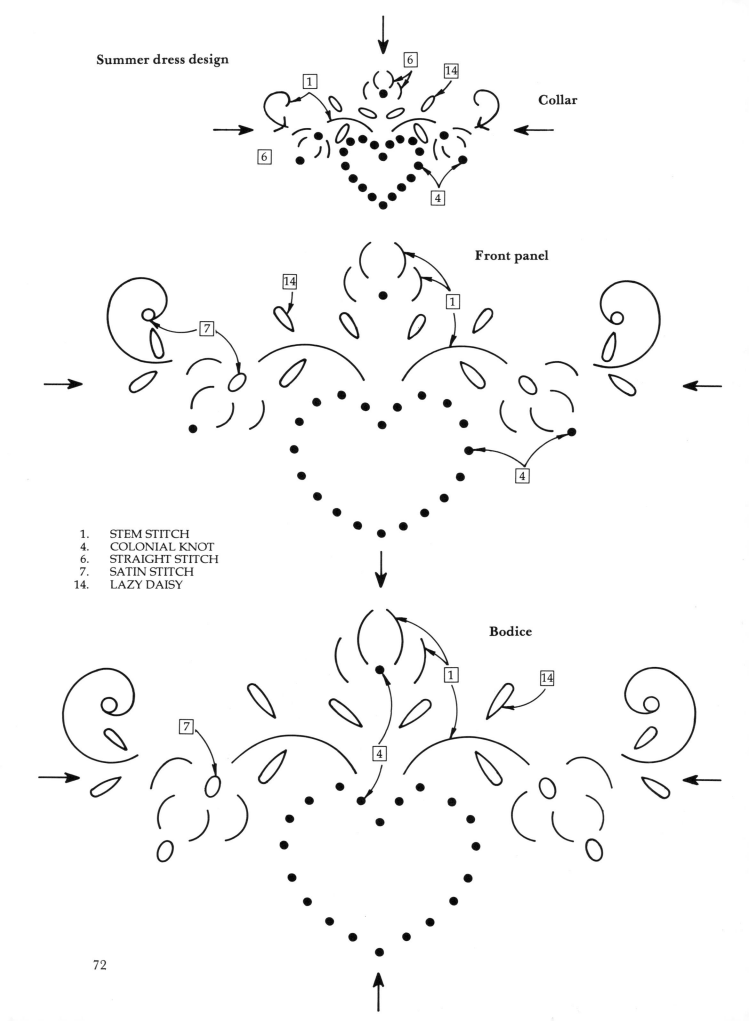

Summer dress design

Collar

Front panel

Bodice

1.   STEM STITCH
4.   COLONIAL KNOT
6.   STRAIGHT STITCH
7.   SATIN STITCH
14. LAZY DAISY

72

Illustrated on page 59

Pillow Cases

Materials

Note: Before cutting the fabric and lace wash following instructions on page 7.

calico or homespun for front of cases, 2 pieces 72 cm × 48 cm (28½'' × 19'')
calico or homespun for back of cases, 4 pieces 48 cm (19'') square
calico or homespun for frills, 4 strips 10 cm × 2.40 m (4'' × 2¾ yds)
double-sided insertion lace, 5 m × 45 mm (5 yds × 1¾'')
satin ribbon, 5 m × 5 mm (5 yds × ¼'')
flat lace, 10 m × 15 mm (10 yds × ⅝'')
tracing paper

1. Trace the design on page 60 onto tracing paper.
2. Fold the fabric front pieces in half horizontally and then vertically, pressing your fingernail across the folds to create crease marks. Match the arrows on the design to the crease lines.
3. Transfer the design from the tracing paper onto the front fabric pieces, following the instructions on page 9. Place the fabric in a hoop and pull the fabric taut.
4. Work the candlewick embroidery on the front fabric pieces.
5. When complete, wash out the blue pen markings in cold water. Allow the fabric to dry, then press with a warm iron.

6. Turn under a 5 mm (¼'') hem and then a 10 mm (½'') hem along one side of the fabric for the backs of the pillow case. Pin, tack and machine stitch.
7. Measure and mark a line 65 mm (2½'') from the raw edge of each of the four sides of the pillowcase.
8. Pin the edge of the insertion lace close to the inside of the line on the short sides first.
9. Tack and machine stitch the lace in place.
10. Thread the ribbon through the lace on both sides of the pillowcase.
11. Follow the same procedure for the long sides.
12. Join two strips of frill together to make a loop. Make a hem around one side of the frill by turning under 5 mm (¼'') and pressing. Turn under 5 mm (¼'') again and press; pin, tack and machine stitch.
13. Sew the 15 mm (⅝'') lace to the right side of the frill as near to the edge as possible.
14. Machine stitch the frill to the front pillowcase, following instructions 2–6 on pages 16–17 (Making a Ruffle and Cushion).
15. With right sides together, pin and tack the pillowcase backings to the front of the pillowcase. Overlap the hemmed backings in the centre. Stitch 5 mm (¼'') around all four sides. Zigzag or overlock around seams and remove tacking thread. Turn the pillowcase right side out.
16. Repeat steps 6–14 for the second pillowcase.

Illustrated on page 61

Dress for Porcelain Doll

This dress is designed for a 79 cm (31'') doll. The pattern pieces will have to be adjusted to fit a larger or smaller doll.

Materials

Note: Before cutting the fabric and lace wash following instructions on page 7.

5 × 7 mm (⅜'') buttons
calico or homespun for dress and petticoat, 1.20 mm × 1 m (1⅜ yd × 1⅛ yd)
gathered cotton lace, 60 cm × 25 mm (23½'' × 1'')
flat cotton lace, 2.20 m × 25 mm (2⅜'' × 1'')
flat cotton lace, 70 cm × 10 mm (27¼'' × ½'')
tracing paper

1. Trace the design from the next page onto tracing paper. Enlarge the patterns on pages 76–77 and copy.
2. Cut a piece 30 cm × 1.10 m (11½'' × 1¼ yds) for the skirt. Cut a piece 27 cm × 1.10 m (10½'' × 1¼ yds) for the petticoat.
3. Transfer the patterns onto the right side of the fabric. Position the centre front panel and the cuffs, measuring 12 cm × 17 cm (4¾'' × 6¾''), close together. Cut all other pieces from the fabric, leaving the front panel and cuffs together. Do not cut these three pieces apart as separately they are too small to fit in a hoop for candlewicking. Centre the design on the front panel. For the cuffs centre the design on the 17 cm (6¾'') edge, the wrist edge. Place the fabric in a hoop and pull taut.
4. Work the candlewick embroidery on the centre front fabric piece and the cuffs.
5. When complete wash out the blue markings with cold water. Allow the fabric to dry and then press with a warm iron.
6. With raw edges matching, stitch gathered lace to both sides of centre front panel.
7. Sew centre front panel to side panels with right sides together, keeping raw edges even and stitching through all thicknesses.
8. With right sides together, stitch bodice front and bodice backs together at shoulder seams.

9. With right sides together, stitch front and back facings together at shoulder seams.
10. With right sides together, pin the 10 mm (½'') lace to the neck edge of dress, keeping raw edges even. Machine stitch.
11. Pin facing to neck edge of dress, right sides together, matching backs and shoulder seams. Machine stitch. Clip curves. Turn the facings to the inside and press the neck edge.
12. Pin sleeve to armhole edge, matching underarm seams. Pull up gathering stitches to fit armhole. Distribute gathers evenly, pin in place and stitch. With right sides together pin sleeves to the top of the cuff, pull up gathering stitches to fit cuff. Distribute gathers evenly. Pin in place and stitch.
13. Pin the 10 mm (½'') lace to the lower edge of cuff and stitch into place. Turn edge to the inside, making a 5 mm (¼'') hem, press and slip stitch the hem.
14. Pin back and front sections together at sides; pin sleeve edges together; pin cuff edges together and stitch in one continuous seam.
15. With right sides together and using a 25 mm (1'') seam allowance, sew centre back seam of skirt. Leave 7 cm (2¾'') of seam open at top of skirt. Repeat the procedure for the petticoat.
16. Pin wrong side of skirt to right side of petticoat at the top edges. Stitch two rows of gathering stitches on top edge of joined skirt and petticoat. Determine centre front of skirt by folding width of skirt in half and mark with a pin. With right sides together, pin skirt to bodice and pull up gathering threads to fit bodice. Sew bodice to skirt. Turn dress wrong side out.
17. Zigzag or overlock back opening edges. Turn back opening edges 10 mm (½'') to inside bodice. Turn facing to inside and slip stitch to centre back edges.
18. Make five 10 mm (½'') buttonholes on the left of bodice back. Sew on buttons.
19. Zigzag or overlock lower edges of skirt and petticoat. Press a 25 mm (1'') hem on the skirt and slip stitch hem. Turn a 5 mm (¼'') hem on the petticoat. Sew the 25 mm (1'') lace around the edge of the petticoat.

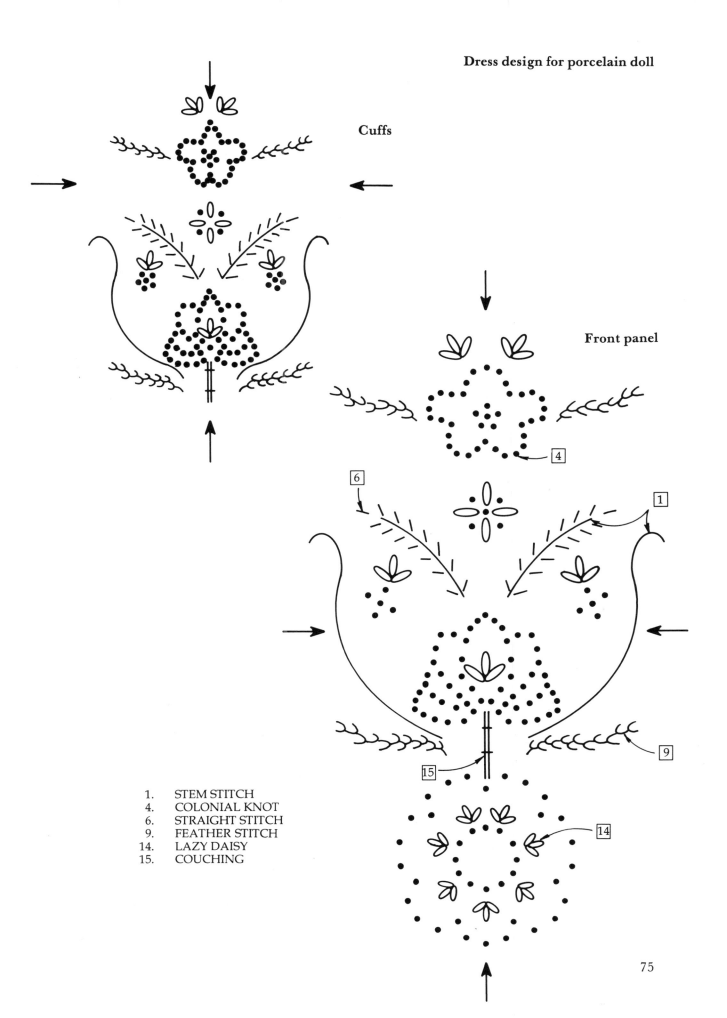

Dress design for porcelain doll

Cuffs

Front panel

1. STEM STITCH
4. COLONIAL KNOT
6. STRAIGHT STITCH
9. FEATHER STITCH
14. LAZY DAISY
15. COUCHING

75

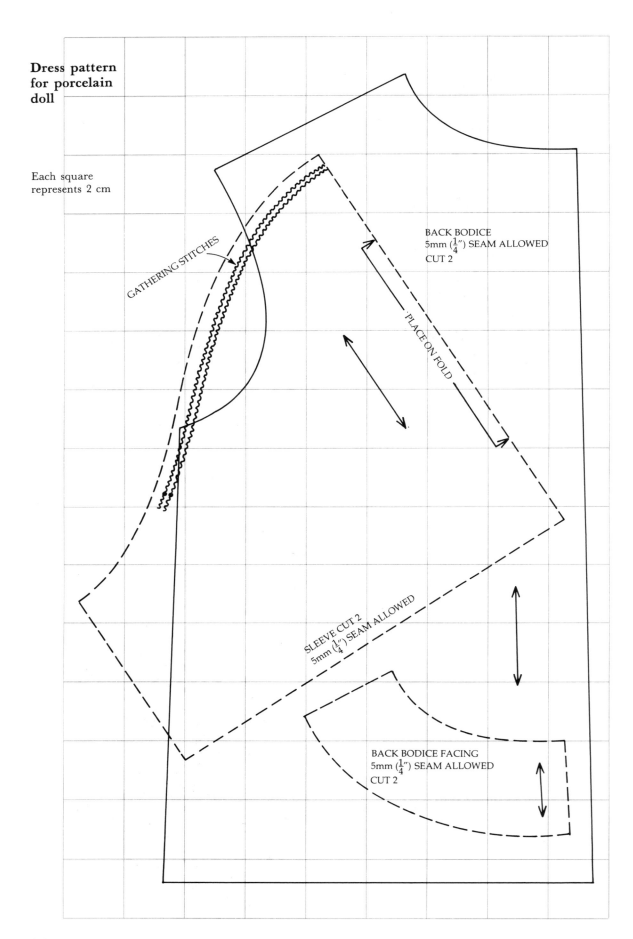

Dress pattern for porcelain doll

Each square represents 2 cm

GATHERING STITCHES

BACK BODICE
5mm ($\frac{1}{4}$″) SEAM ALLOWED
CUT 2

PLACE ON FOLD

SLEEVE CUT 2
5mm ($\frac{1}{4}$″) SEAM ALLOWED

BACK BODICE FACING
5mm ($\frac{1}{4}$″) SEAM ALLOWED
CUT 2

76

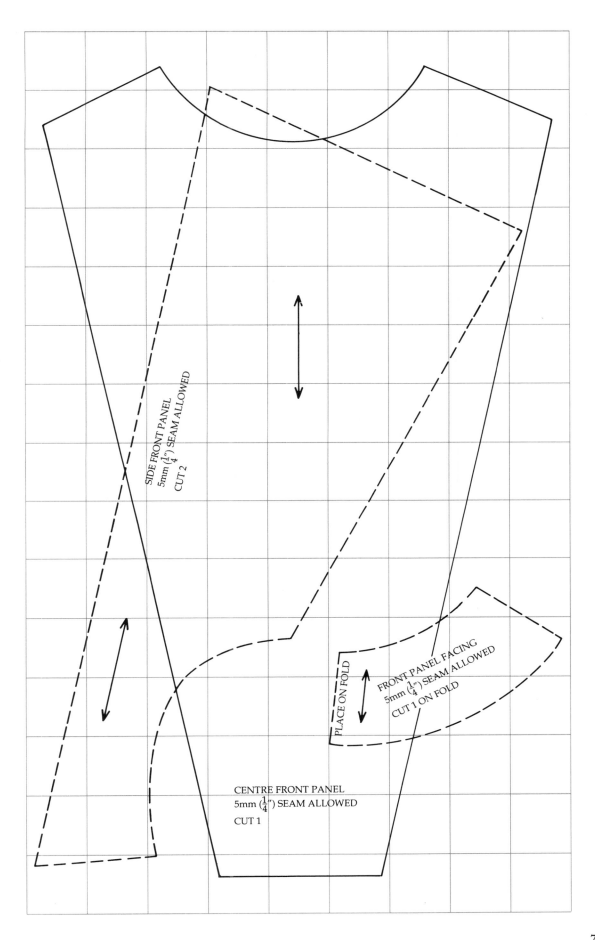

SIDE FRONT PANEL
5mm ($\frac{1}{4}$") SEAM ALLOWED
CUT 2

FRONT PANEL FACING
5mm ($\frac{1}{4}$") SEAM ALLOWED
CUT 1 ON FOLD

PLACE ON FOLD

CENTRE FRONT PANEL
5mm ($\frac{1}{4}$") SEAM ALLOWED
CUT 1

Illustrated on page 61

Coathanger

Materials

Note: Before cutting the fabric and lace wash following instructions on page 7.

calico or homespun, 40 cm × 60 cm (15¾'' × 23¾'')
apparel wadding, 40 cm × 60 cm (15¾'' × 23¾'')
braid, 60 cm × 5 mm (23¾'' × ¼'')
gathered lace, 45 cm × 3 cm (17¾'' × 1¼'')
satin ribbon, 50 cm × 5 mm (20'' × ¼'')
plastic-coated coathanger
polyester stuffing
tracing paper

1. Trace the pattern and design on the next page onto tracing paper.
2. Cut two pieces of wadding from the hanger pattern.
3. Transfer back and front coathanger patterns and design from the tracing paper onto the right side of fabric, following the instructions on page 9. *Do not cut out.* It will be very difficult to candlewick on the edge.
4. Work the candlewick embroidery on the front piece of the coathanger.

5. When complete cut out the pattern pieces and wash in cold water to remove the blue pen markings. Allow the fabric to dry and press with a warm iron.
6. Pin, tack and machine stitch the lace, right sides and raw edges together, to the bottom of the front fabric.
7. With right sides together place backing fabric on front fabric. Place one piece of wadding on wrong side of backing fabric. Place the other piece of wadding on the wrong side of front fabric. Pin and tack all four pieces together.
8. Machine stitch both sides of coathanger, stitching from the base to the hook and leaving a 10 mm (½'') opening at the hook. Remove the tacking.
9. Turn right sides out. Fold the raw edges at the base of the coathanger, 5 mm (¼'') inside the hanger and press to create a 5 mm (¼'') seam.
10. Insert the hanger and stuff with polyester stuffing. Slip stitch the opening closed.
11. Cover hook with braid, starting at the tip, and glue in place. Wrap the braid around the hook and tuck any overhang into the coathanger cover. Slip stitch the opening closed.
12. Tie a bow at the base of the hook.

Coathanger pattern and design

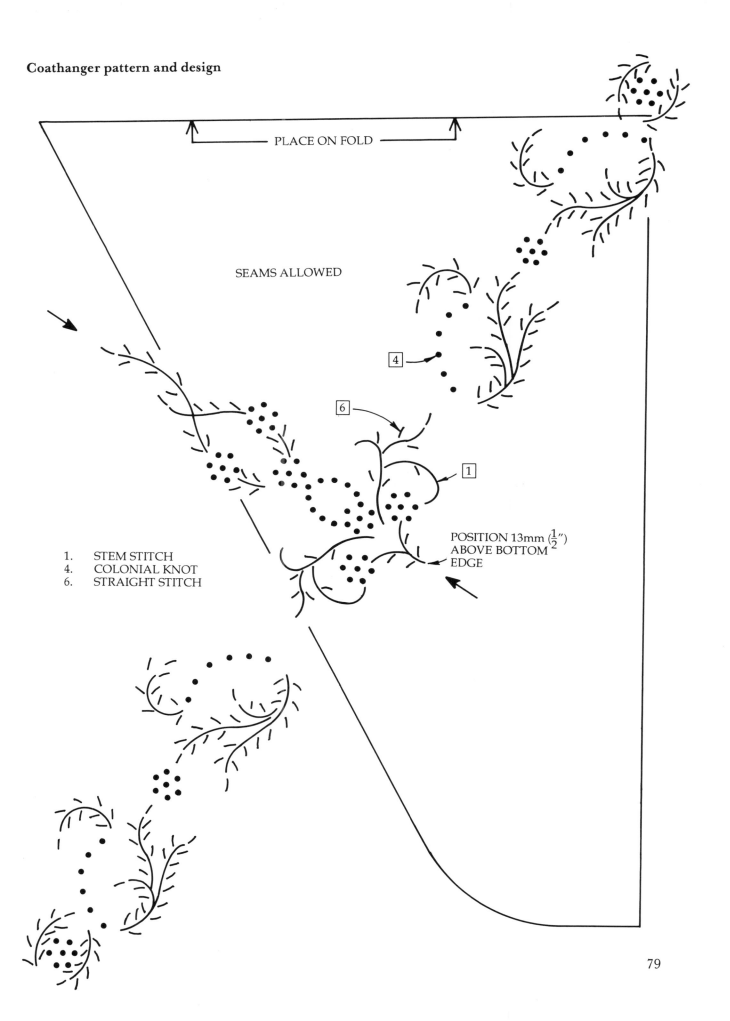

PLACE ON FOLD

SEAMS ALLOWED

4

6

1

POSITION 13mm ($\frac{1}{2}$")
ABOVE BOTTOM
EDGE

1.   STEM STITCH
4.   COLONIAL KNOT
6.   STRAIGHT STITCH

79

THE GARDEN

Illustrated on page 63

Rose Pruning Gloves

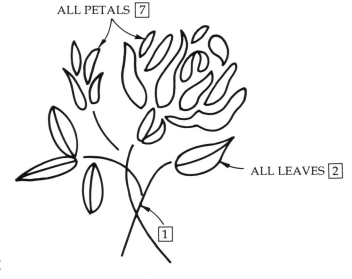

ALL PETALS [7]

ALL LEAVES [2]

[1]

Materials
1 pair gardening gloves
tracing paper
washable transfer pencil

1. Trace the design onto tracing paper.
2. Trace the outline of the design on the tracing paper with the transfer pencil, remembering to reverse the design for the second glove.
3. Iron the design onto the gloves.
4. Work the candlewick embroidery on the front piece of each glove.
5. Wash out the transfer pencil in cold water, dry gloves and press carefully with a warm iron.

1. STEM STITCH
2. FISHBONE STITCH
7. SATIN STITCH

Illustrated on page 63

Table Cloth

Materials

Note: Before cutting the fabric and lace wash following instructions on page 7.

calico or homespun, 1.05 m (41'') square
flat cotton lace, 4.50 m × 7 cm (5 yds × 2¾'')
tracing paper

1. Trace the design from the next page onto tracing paper.
2. Following the instructions on the design, match the corners of the fabric with the design on the tracing paper and trace the design onto all four corners.

3. Place the corners one at a time in a hoop and pull the fabric taut.
4. Work the candlewick embroidery on the front pieces.
5. When complete wash out blue pen markings with cold water. Allow the fabric to dry, then carefully press with a warm iron.
6. Machine stitch a mitred hem around all four sides following instructions on page 15.
7. Stitch cotton lace around all four sides, mitring the corners following instructions on page 15.

Table cloth design

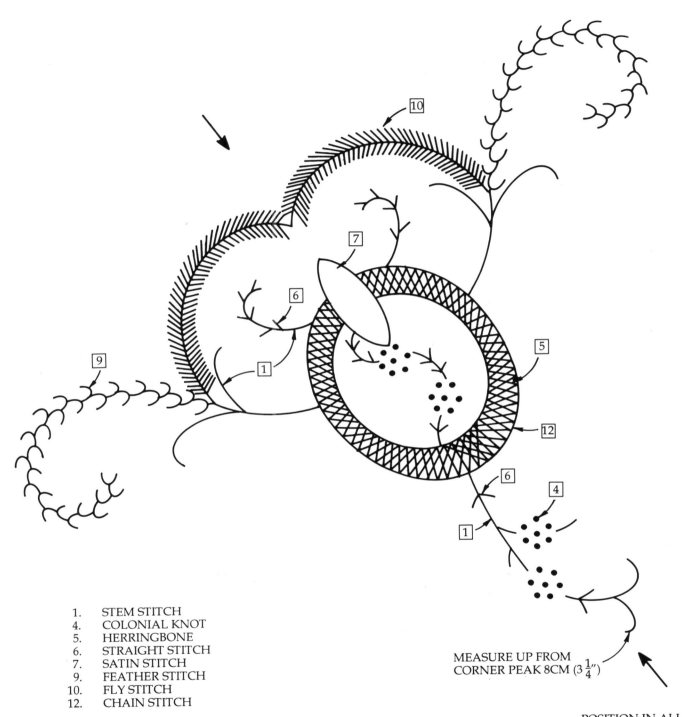

1. STEM STITCH
4. COLONIAL KNOT
5. HERRINGBONE
6. STRAIGHT STITCH
7. SATIN STITCH
9. FEATHER STITCH
10. FLY STITCH
12. CHAIN STITCH

MEASURE UP FROM
CORNER PEAK 8CM (3$\frac{1}{4}$″)

POSITION IN ALL
FOUR CORNERS

Teapot Cosy

Materials

Note: Before cutting the fabric and lace wash following instructions on page 7.

calico or homespun for front and backing, 2 pieces 40 cm × 25 cm (16'' × 10'')
apparel wadding, 40 cm × 25 cm (16'' × 10'')
satin ribbon, 4 pieces 30 cm × 10 mm (11½'' × ⅜'')
gathered lace, 90 cm × 3 cm (1 yd × 1¼'')
tracing paper

1. Trace the design on page 57 onto tracing paper.
2. Fold the front fabric in half vertically so that it measures 40 cm × 12.5 cm (16'' × 5''). Press with your fingernail across the fold to create a crease line. Match the arrows on the design with the crease line. Position the design 5 cm (2'') up from the base of the cosy; pin the fabric and paper together.
3. Transfer the design from the tracing paper onto the front fabric following the instructions on page 9. Transfer onto the other side in the same manner.
4. Tack the wadding to the wrong side of the front fabric, place the front piece in the hoop and pull taut.

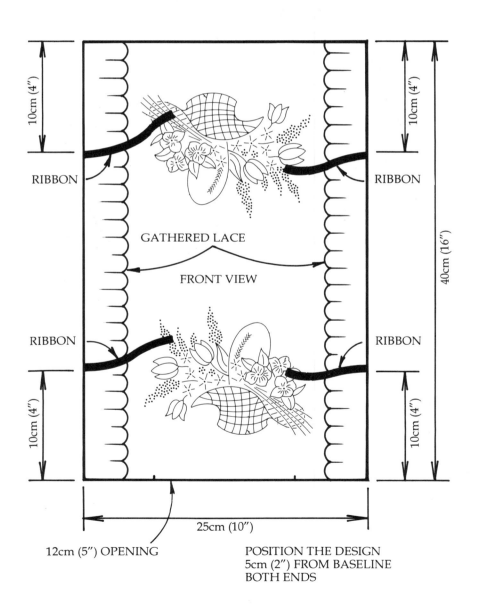

10cm (4")

RIBBON

GATHERED LACE

FRONT VIEW

RIBBON

40cm (16")

10cm (4")

RIBBON

10cm (4")

10cm (4")

RIBBON

25cm (10")

12cm (5") OPENING

POSITION THE DESIGN
5cm (2") FROM BASELINE
BOTH ENDS

5. Work the candlewick embroidery on both sides.
6. When complete wash out the blue pen markings in cold water. Allow the fabric to dry then press with a warm iron.
7. Cut the gathered lace in half. Pin right sides and raw edges of lace and long sides of the cosy together. Position the four ribbons as shown (Figure 1) and pin. Tack and machine stitch close to raw edges.
8. With right sides together pin and tack the backing to the front. Machine stitch a 5 mm (¼'') seam

around the edge, leaving a 12 cm (5'') opening in the centre of one end for turning through.
9. Zigzag or overlock seams. Clip corners and remove tacking. Turn right side out.
10. Fold the raw edges at the opening 5 mm (¼'') inside the tea cosy and press to create a neat seam. Neatly slip stitch the opening closed. Remove all remaining tacking on the cosy. Press carefully with a warm iron.

Illustrated on page 64

Scone Warmer

Materials

Note: Before cutting the fabric and lace wash following instructions on page 7.

calico or homespun for front and backing, 2 circles 60 cm (23½'') in diameter
flat lace, 2 m × 10 mm (2¼ yds × ½'')
braid, 4 m × 3 mm (4⅜ yds × ⅛'')
tracing paper

1. Trace the design below onto tracing paper.
2. Fold the front circle of fabric in half (Figure 1), then in half again. Press firmly (Figure 2) to form four quarters (Figure 3).

3. Transfer the design on the tracing paper onto the fabric four times, following the instructions on page 9. Place the front fabric in a hoop and pull taut.
4. Work the candlewick embroidery on the front fabric.
5. When complete wash out blue pen markings in cold water. Allow the fabric to dry, then press carefully with a warm iron.
6. Fold the front circle in half and make two buttonholes on the crease line 35 mm in from the edge of the circle, as shown in Figure 4. Carefully slit the buttonholes.
7. On the right side of the backing circle draw two lines with the blue water-soluble pen 3 cm (1¼'') and 5 cm (2'') in from the edges (Figure 5). This will form the casing for the braid.

Scone warmer design

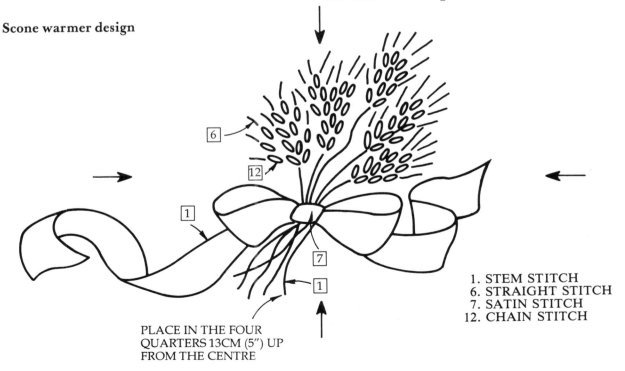

PLACE IN THE FOUR
QUARTERS 13CM (5") UP
FROM THE CENTRE

1. STEM STITCH
6. STRAIGHT STITCH
7. SATIN STITCH
12. CHAIN STITCH

8. Place both circles right sides together, tack and machine stitch 5 mm (¼'') in from the raw edge of the fabric, leaving a 10 cm (4'') opening for turning through. Remove tacking.

9. Turn the fabric through the opening, press the raw edges at the opening 5 mm (¼'') inside the warmer to create a neat seam. Neatly slip stitch the opening closed.

10. Machine stitch along the lines drawn in Instruction 7.

11. Cut the braid in half. Using a safety pin thread one piece in through one buttonhole, around the full circle and out through the same buttonhole (Figure 6). Tie the ends together. Using the same procedure, thread the other piece of braid in through the opposite buttonhole.

12. Pull the braids at the knots to draw the fabric up into a pouch.

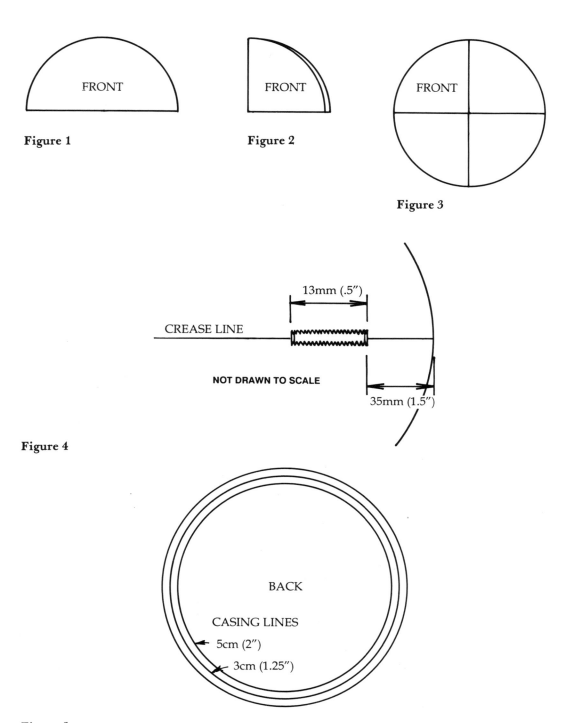

FRONT

Figure 1

FRONT

Figure 2

FRONT

Figure 3

CREASE LINE

13mm (.5'')

NOT DRAWN TO SCALE

35mm (1.5'')

Figure 4

BACK

CASING LINES

5cm (2'')

3cm (1.25'')

Figure 5

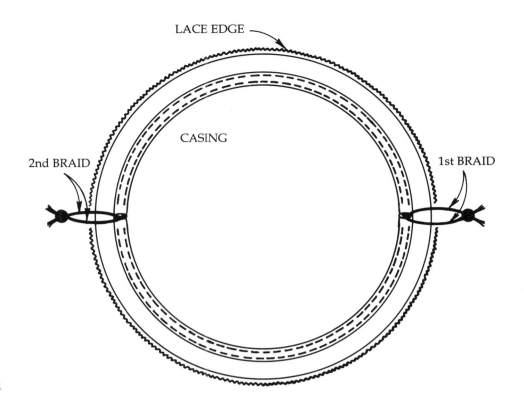

Figure 6

Index